Teamwork &
Indian Culture

A Practical Guide for Working with Indians

Revised Edition

Thota Ramesh

www.ThoDu.org

DEDICATION

This book is dedicated to THREE most influential persons in my life:

To my father Late Sri. Thota Durgaiah
To my brother-in-law Prof. Dr. M. Prabhakar
To my brother Lt. Col (Dr) T. Dayakar

Contents

Preface

[**Note for the Revised Edition:** *This Revised edition includes a new chapter "Chalta-hai" replacing the chapter "Heading Home". I must confess that being an Indian I also have this attitude; and it was reflected in many English language errors in the earlier print. In this version, I tried my best to correct them.*]

This book evolved out of a seminar I gave in 2005 at Hyderabad-SPIN (Software Process Improvement Network) meeting. The title of the seminar was "Indian Culture and its impact on Teamwork." In that seminar, I have shared my views about teamwork culture in India. The main message was that in India, the individuals' aspirations come in the way of achieving team's goals. This lack of teamwork is affecting India in every facet of life, e.g. not getting enough medals in Olympics.

I am sure you will agree with me that the success of a project is dependent on the teamwork. In this book, I am going to elaborate on those issues that play a significant role on the teamwork in India.

As an Indian and as a practicing Project Manager for the last 20 years, I realized the significance of the role of culture in teamwork. When things were going wrong with the team, I used to think it as the personality problems of the individuals.

As I tried to understand the behavior of the people more deeply, I found an underlying pattern. I have effectively brought change in my teams by carefully working on those behavior patterns which were working against the team. I am going to share those observations with you in this book. Hope it makes it easy for you to understand Indian teamwork culture better and helps you achieve your team's goals.

The importance of teamwork is more evident in an organization's success. I attribute the success of IT giant Infosys to the teamwork of Sri. N.R. Narayana Murthy & Co. The same is true about ADP India Pvt. Ltd. Thanks to late Sri Balaji, I had the opportunity to work closely with this great team of Shakti Sagar, Thiagarajan (Tiger), VLK, Ganesan and Balaji. In my opinion, both these teams are the epitome of teamwork.

___***___

The Maiden Voyage

"Welcome to Hyderabad! The local time is 5:45 AM…" announced the Air-India hostess. John was pleased to hear the announcement and felt relieved. This was the first time he had traveled outside of America, and it was the longest air travel. He was nervous and little scared throughout this journey of 23 hours. He had mixed feelings - he was happy to have landed safely and excited yet anxious about visiting a new country, India.

He remembered the day his boss Mike called him and said, "John, are you ready for an adventure?" Before he could answer, Mike continued, "You are our expert on 'strategic pricing'. In this recession, it is important that we beat our competitors on price at every level. We want you to build a software application which can help us react instantaneously to the price changes of our competitors. We have decided to get this developed in our Hyderabad unit." Mike paused for a moment and continued, "So, I want you to fly over to India and get this system built in the next six months. Are you ready?"

John was taken aback by that sudden instruction. As a Business Analyst, he had been interacting with the teams in India and had also spoken to the Hyderabad location head Vinod Mehta recently. He had very pleasant feelings about the team in India and was quite appreciative of their work. However, traveling to India and working there for six months appeared to him as a tall order. He had never gone out of America. Going to a place on the other side of the globe seemed quite challenging yet disturbing. On the other hand, he heard a lot about India – its past, its culture, its present. It was once-in-a-life-time opportunity to live in India. Many of his colleagues, who love traveling, have the desire to visit India. He thought it would be great fun to live there than just visit. He sought time from Mike to think about it.

"Excuse me!" John was jolted back to reality, when the passenger sitting next to him wanted to open the overhead bin. He stood up; picked up the book he was reading during the flight and his cabin baggage; and proceeded towards the door. On the way out of the plane and onto aerobridge, he nonchalantly gestured good-bye to the air hostess's 'Namaste'.

"Wow!" John said to himself after looking at the Hyderabad International Airport. He was not expecting such a modern airport even though he heard that it was built recently. He made his way through the immigration & customs. During that time, he realized that there were quite a good number of westerners like him in the airport. It gave him a sense of relief and comfort. He arranged his baggage on the trolley, put all his papers safely into his brief case, took a deep breath and said to himself, "John! You are here in India! Get ready for the adventure."

"Hi John!"

John stopped pushing his cart when he heard his name. He was told someone from his company would meet him at the airport. He noticed an Indian in his forties waving at him. He gave a sigh of relief as so many things were going through his mind about the consequences of someone not showing up. He smiled, moved towards him and tried to do "Namaste" – the way it was mentioned in the book on India. Before he could do that, the man extended his hand for shaking and gave a gentle hug.

"John! I am Dheeraj. Good to see you. How was your trip?"

"Hi, it was good. It is such a long journey, but was good. Thanks for coming."

"No problem. All arrangements are made for your comfortable stay. Let me help you with your cart."

John tried to object, but Dheeraj insisted saying, "You must have been very tired and above all, you are our guest & friend. Let me help," - with a smile, he pointed to the 'India Tourism' poster. Dheeraj took the cart, handed over the briefcase and laptop to him. John was very pleased with that gesture. He was used to doing all his work on his own. He believed in each person taking care of himself – without the help of others. He was happy to see Dheeraj – to whom he would be reporting - personally coming to the airport to receive him.

As they stepped out of the Airport Arrivals, John noticed many people holding the placards with the names of the guests. He also noticed many passengers straining their necks in search of the placard displaying their names. He was glad that he did not have to go through all this. Both made their way out of the airport fast, as Dheeraj skillfully pushed the cart through the maze of people.

As they approached a waiting Scorpio, they were received with a 'Namaste Sir' by a well-dressed driver, Venkat. Venkat took the brief case, laptop from John and took charge of the cart. Dheeraj motioned John to get into the vehicle. John took out his coat and boarded the vehicle.

"It is so pleasant. What could be the temperature now?"

"Around 25 degrees"

"25 degrees! It is same as the temperature in my city?"

"25 degrees Celsius, not Fahrenheit. In Fahrenheit, it will be around 75"

"Oh! I get it."

"Shall we start now, Sir?" asked Venkat. He was already in his driver's seat after safely loading the baggage. Dheeraj gestured at him to start. The Scorpio started off smoothly.

John stretched his legs, leaned back to relax. So many thoughts were going through his head. It was all appearing like a dream for him. Just in one day, he flew across the globe and landed in a completely different country & continent. The vehicle was zipping past open fields, widely dispersed houses and occasional automobiles. He had so many concerns about visiting India. He was very pleased with his experiences so far.

Dheeraj enquired with John about Mike and other team members in USA. He started briefing John about Hyderabad and the office. He pointed to the flyover they were traveling on and said, "John, the flyover we are on is India's longest flyover. It is 12 kilo meters." Reacting to the look on John's face, he said, "7.5 miles"

Dheeraj continued his briefing about Hyderabad and stopped when he noticed that John had fallen asleep. Dheeraj also closed his eyes to relax.

"Screeeeeeeeeeeech!.........". Sudden stop of the vehicle jolted both out of their relaxation. John looked at front and noticed a yellow color vehicle blocking their vehicle. It was a three-wheeler. And he saw some children inside and many school bags hanging outside. Luckily, there was no accident. John looked around. They had already crossed the flyover and were on a main road. There were many vehicles stalled in front of theirs. He was amazed to see many different vehicles – three wheelers, bicycles, motorcycles, buses, trucks, small cars – all sharing the same road. Suddenly, he remembered the Indian scene from one of the James Bond movies. Their vehicle started moving very slowly. John was completely engrossed in watching the roadside. He had never seen such a scene in his life. Along the road, there were shops, buildings, houses. Each one was unique and colorful. There were many hoardings all over the buildings, on trees and on the electrical poles.

As they approached the crossroads, he saw the traffic red lights blinking. To a question by Dheeraj, Venkat replied that traffic lights would start functioning from 8 AM. They were in the middle of the traffic junction, and all around them were vehicles. Each one was competing with others to inch ahead. People were gesturing, shouting and pushing their way out of the traffic jam.

Venkat and Dheeraj lowered their windows. The sudden burst of loud noise jolted John. He did not realize the noise levels outside of his closed vehicle. He was amused at watching all that was going on. He was wondering if they would ever come out of that jam. Both Venkat and Dheeraj leaned out of their windows and started requesting the people around to make way for them. After a few anxious moments, they could wade out of the traffic jam and reach their hotel safely. It was so entertaining for John. Now he was completely awake and feeling refreshed.

Dheeraj helped John check-in to the reserved room. He gave some instructions to John about the catering and ordering system in the hotel. He gave his business card and scribbled his mobile number on it. He gave the contact numbers of company's admin staff too, in case he needs any help.

John was eager to visit the office. However Dheeraj asked him to take rest for one full day to overcome the jet lag.

"Relax today, John. Tomorrow, Venkat will come to pick you up at 8:30 AM. See you tomorrow."

"Bye. Thanks for everything," said John while shaking Dheeraj's hand.

---***---

Meeting the Team

Next-day morning, John was ready and waiting for Venkat. At sharp 8:26 AM Venkat entered the lobby of the hotel. John approached him and said,

"Hi Venkat," greeted John.

"Good morning sir," replied Venkat and offered to pick up John's laptop. John gestured 'No', and both left the hotel and got into Scorpio.

Resting for a whole day after the long journey had really helped John. John appreciated Dheeraj for the advice. The facilities at the hotel were top class, and the service was exceptional. They helped him relax well. He was now completely refreshed and eager to start his work.

John noticed that they were out of the hotel complex and on the main road. John lowered his tinted window to have a better look at the surroundings. Cool, pleasant morning breeze greeted him. The noise levels on that road were low. The traffic was moving smoothly. It appeared to him that they were in the outskirts of the city. He noticed vast dry fields on both sides of the road with houses spread sparsely. After every two miles are so, there were clusters of houses, buildings and shops – most of them closed. He noticed small shanty places having hoardings with the words 'Tiffin Center' written in English and in local language. He also noticed few people sitting there sipping tea and having breakfast.

The drive was smooth. The breeze was pleasant. Once again, the visuals around appeared to be from a James Bond movie. All this felt surreal to John. As he looked into the distance, beautiful buildings with lush green lawns and plenty of trees caught the attention of his eyes. As their vehicle drove nearer, he saw sprawling campuses with modern buildings surrounded with well maintained landscapes. These appeared to him as Oases in a desert. He immediately recognized them as the campuses of major IT firms – confirmed by the hoardings boldly showing the names of 'Wipro', 'Infosys', 'TCS' and others.

The Scorpio took them onto another main road lined up with multi-storied buildings. There were many buses and cars parked on either side of the road. There was a sea of humanity of well-dressed young men and women crossing the road. Venkat drove the vehicle cautiously and took a left turn onto a small road facing a huge complex 'Cyber Gateway'. The name rang a bell in John's mind. Immediately, he pulled out a note from his pocket and looked at the address to confirm. It was a very impressive multi-storied modern building. Every building there appeared to be competing with each other in elegance and design.

The security guards at the gate stopped the vehicle. They talked to Venkat and inspected the vehicle before letting them into the complex. Venkat dropped John at the lobby entrance after explaining him the directions to his office.

As John entered the lobby, he noticed the names 'Oracle', 'Dell', 'GE', 'Microsoft' on the list of companies. He had to pass through the security check at the lobby to reach the elevators. He took the elevator and found the office. As he walked into the office, the lady behind the reception had asked him to sign in. She was warm and pointed him to the small neat corner where coffee vending machines were installed and asked him to help himself.

John found his favorite coffee and felt at home. Sipping at it, he looked around and was very impressed by the posh interiors of the reception. The earlier image he had of India came to his mind – a poor nation with buffaloes on the road, beggars on the street. While thinking back, he just remembered seeing few shanty structures across the road and opposite to this huge complex. He remembered seeing many people - with different dress styles, some men half-naked - huddling at those places and having food. He did not see such a major contrast anywhere in US, world-class structures and shanty structures next to each other.

"Hi John!"

"Good Morning, Dheeraj," said John extending his hand. Dheeraj shook his hand and gave a friendly hug.

"Welcome to Hyderabad office. Hope you had a good rest at the hotel." Dheeraj put his hand around John's shoulder and escorted him to the office. John noticed the familiar setting – cubicles, workstations and the Conference rooms. Dheeraj opened the door to his cabin and invited John inside. It was spacious and well maintained. There was a whiteboard on the wall, a sofa against the wall, and three chairs in front of Dheeraj's desk. Dheeraj motioned John to take one of those seats and settled into his chair.

"John, we have earmarked a cabin for you to use throughout your stay here. By the way, based on our earlier discussions, I have identified a team for you. Let me know what other resources you need."

John started explaining the project, timelines and the resources he needed. He used the white-board between the discussions to explain few points. The discussion went on for half an hour with Dheeraj noting down few points.

At the end of it, Dheeraj said, "Excellent! John, glad to see the clarity you have on all aspects of this project. Rest assured I will provide all the support you need to succeed in this. Feel free to ask me about anything you need. I am here to help you succeed."

John was happy to hear this. This was his first project as a Project Manager. So far, he had been playing the role of a Business Analyst for various projects. On occasions, he acted as Project Manager, whenever the assigned Project Manager was not available. He whole heartedly said, "Thank you, Dheeraj" and shook Dheeraj's hand.

"You are most welcome. Enjoy your stay here," said Dheeraj.

"I have a question for you," said John and waited for Dheeraj's reaction. He continued once Dheeraj nodded his head approvingly.

"Can I call you Raj? I am having difficulty in pronouncing your name."

Dheeraj just became aware how John was pronouncing his name. He was calling him 'Dhi-rawj'. With a smile, Dheeraj said, "I will help you with my name. I prefer to be called Dheeraj. The 'raj' in 'Dheeraj'; and 'Raj' in 'Raj' are pronounced differently even though the spelling is same. We don't have that confusion when we write our names in Indian languages as almost all of them are phonetic based. Unfortunately, English is not so. Maybe, we should start printing the phonetic version on the back of our business cards."

He pronounced his name slowly and explained.

"The first syllable 'Dhee' rhymes with 'Thee'; and the 'R-a' in 'raj' is pronounced as the 'R-u' as in 'Rug'. Every Indian name has a specific meaning. The independent word 'Raj' means king. The meaning of Dheeraj in my native language Telugu is bravery. The same word in Hindi means patience."

John remembered from the book on India that every state in India has its own language, and Hindi is its national language. He wondered how the Indians learn three languages so effectively.

Dheeraj continued, "Mispronouncing a name can lead to entirely different meaning, sometimes it can be offensive too."

"Wow! I am glad you explained this to me. I will practice hard getting the names right," said John smilingly. On hearing a knock on the door, he turned his head and looked back. He saw a pretty young lady standing in the doorway. She is wearing a colorful Indian dress.

"Good morning, Sir!" she said to Dheeraj.

"Good morning, come in," said Dheeraj rising from his chair. Turning towards John, who was also on his feet by then, he said, "John, she is Nasreen. Nasreen, this is John."

Nasreen looked at John and said, "Hi!" with a little bow.

"Hi!" replied John.

"She is your project leader. I have already given her a brief about you. She will show you around this office and introduce you to the team"

"Nasreen, what time is the meeting?" asked Dheeraj.

"After tea-time, at 11:00 AM"

"Ok. I will join you guys at that time"

John got the cue and followed Nasreen to take a tour of the facilities.

John found Nasreen to be very composed and dignified. She took him first to his assigned office, so that he could leave his laptop and other belongings there. She then introduced him to the important admin staff, helped him pick up some stationery; showed the canteen, gym and left him at his office.

John unpacked his stuff, looked at his family photo for a while and placed it on his table after hesitating a little. On his tour of the facilities, he did not see any photos on the desks. He did not remember seeing any either in Dheeraj's room.

He set up his laptop and started preparing for his first meeting with the team. He did not realize that it was time for the meeting until he heard a knock at his door. It was Dheeraj. Together they went to the meeting room where the team was already waiting for them. As they entered, some of the team members were about to stand up. Dheeraj motioned at them to sit down and gestured John to take a seat. He introduced John, gave a brief about the project and asked them to extend their full cooperation to him.

"John, let us meet at 4 PM in my office to review your day," said Dheeraj.

"Sure, I will be there after the tea time," replied John, stressing the words 'tea time'. He came to know through Nasreen about the breaks called 'tea time'. In the morning tea time, he saw almost entire staff in the canteen.

On Dheeraj's leaving, Nasreen started introducing every team member to John. In the meantime, John hooked up his laptop to the projection system and kept his Power point presentation ready. After the introductions, John stood up and explained the project.

During his presentation, John stopped a couple of times when he noticed the team members discussing with each other.

He asked, "Do you have any questions?"

"No, sir!" came the reply promptly every time.

He asked the team if everyone had understood what he was presenting.

"Yes, sir!" came the reply in unison.

ॐ

It was 4 PM. Dheeraj and John were sitting in the canteen near the glass walls. The view outside was beautiful with the majestic buildings and sprawling campuses of other companies. The sun was still bright. The roads were busy with the traffic.

John was excited over the events of the day. He was no longer feeling like a stranger. He was eager to share all that happened with Dheeraj.

"How did everything go, John?" asked Dheeraj.

"It is great. Thanks for making all the arrangements. I like Nasreen. She is very intelligent and helpful. I am yet to know the other team members individually, but they all seemed to grasp the things pretty fast."

"Ok"

"I had trouble initially, when they were nodding their heads in response to my questions. I could not find out if it is 'Yes' or 'No'. It is different from the way I am used to. Now I know the difference."

"By the way," continued John, "I have asked them not to call me 'sir'. Quite a few of them were referring to me as 'sir'. It is embarrassing. I asked them to address me by my first name 'John'."

"Yes. We tend to call everyone above in the hierarchy as 'Sir' or 'Madam'," said Dheeraj leaning forward.

John realized that he would get an elaborate explanation on this. He started enjoying the conversations with Dheeraj. He liked the way Dheeraj explained about the names. When he met the team, he was extra cautious in pronouncing their names. He had jotted down the pronunciation against each team member's name in his note pad - against Nasreen's name he had written 'Nuz-rean'.

"Apart from the persons of authority, every elder person is also treated with reverence. We don't address elder persons by their first names as it is considered bad manners. For example, my niece who is just one year younger to me…."

"Your niece, just one year younger?" exclaimed John.

"Yes, ours is a big family. She is the daughter of my eldest brother. She addresses me as 'Uncle'. And we address our neighbors 'Uncle', 'Aunt', 'Brother', 'Sister' even though they are not a family relation. In our tradition, we have to respect every elder, and we love to retain it – it is our culture. Irrespective of our age, we are a child to an elder always. The Parent-Child relationship pervades all the interactions we have with elders and authority figures. We are conditioned from our childhood to desist from addressing elders and seniors by their first names. If we have to refer to the name of an elder, we suffix it with 'garu' in Telugu or 'ji' in Hindi, akin to 'Esq' to show respect."

John recollected Nasreen referring to Dheeraj as 'Dheeraj garu'.

"The IT revolution has brought in this culture of addressing each other by their first names," continued Dheeraj. "Now, it has percolated to other industries also. Twenty years ago, it was a sort of cultural shock for me. I struggled hard to avoid the situations that involve me using the first names of elders. Even now, many who are new to the industry go through the same problem."

Dheeraj paused to sip his tea and then continued, "At professional settings, many argue that it makes sense to cultivate this habit. This will make everyone, irrespective of his position, to interact with everyone else on a level field. It will encourage the Adult-to-Adult interactions. I personally feel we can retain the Indian culture of 'not addressing elders by their first names' and still maintain Adult-to-Adult interactions. The main idea here is to be democratic rather than autocratic. This in turn will make every interaction and every discussion more rational and productive. It is the cornerstone for building an effective team, where each individual can contribute positively to the team's goals."

Dheeraj looked at John and continued, "We communicate this as part of our induction training for new employees. But, the rules outside of the industry conflict with this, so we don't get to see 100% compliance. It becomes individual manager's responsibility to inculcate the same. I am glad you did that on the first interaction itself. As western culture advocates first name usage, the team members have to adapt to both cultures and strike a balance."

John was awed by that explanation. That behavior appeared so simple at the outset, but it was really a complex thing. He could empathize with the difficulty associated with balancing the conflicting rules of social engagement.

The discussion went on to the other experiences of John which he described animatedly. Especially, he had lots of praise for the team for their enthusiasm and their ability to understand the project. Every time he checked with them if they could follow him or not, he got the affirmative answer 'Yes'. That had made him feel good.

Dheeraj listened to John attentively and appreciated him for the good beginning.

"Great John, I am happy that your first day went very well. You can stop by my office any time you need my help. Best wishes."

Dheeraj patted John affectionately, and both left for their cabins.

---***---

Yes Sir! Yes Madam!

One week passed. It was 4 PM; both John & Dheeraj were sitting in their favorite place in the canteen. John's face was grim. That day, he had asked one of the team members to explain the overall functionality he had presented. To his dismay, he found the team member's understanding was completely wrong. John asked the rest of the team to help. Their understanding was no different. All the while, John thought he was very effective in communication. He thought he ensured that everyone got a clear understanding of the project. But now he felt that he was back at the beginning. Here, he was with Dheeraj to understand what went wrong. He explained to Dheeraj about the daily sessions on the project functionality. And gave a brief about what he had covered so far. With a shrug of his shoulders and throwing up his arms in despair, he continued,

"I can't make out what went wrong. I have been preparing for these sessions for quite some time. I have gone to a great extent to explain every concept in detail. I thought I ensured that everyone has understood them clearly. But….." he paused for a while.

"......but, today I realized that many of them did not understand the basic concepts. I have to start all over again. Until today morning, I was so excited about this team. Yesterday, I told Mike that the team was doing well and at this pace we might complete the project earlier than originally planned. I am at loss to understand how I have misjudged," said John slumping into his seat.

Dheeraj could empathize with him. He decided to comfort John first and then get to the bottom of the situation.

"Relax John. I understand how much you value this project and how important it is for you. I am glad you have found a problem at this early stage. You deserve compliments. The earlier we find a problem, the better it is for the project. I think you were one of the very few managers, who had come back to me for help so early in the project. I appreciate you for your initiative to correct the things." These words had a positive effect on John. He sat upright and leaned forward to listen carefully.

Dheeraj noticed the change and said, "You are jumping to conclusions too fast. I know this is the first assignment for you as a Project Manager, and you are excited. But, don't worry about the project deadlines at this stage. Try getting to know the team well. You seem to have a communication problem with the team"

John interjected, "I don't see any issue with the communication. They understand and speak English very well. To ensure proper communication, I asked them quite often if they understood. Every time, I got the answer 'Yes'…"

"And…. you have taken it for granted that they understood everything you presented," commented Dheeraj. "The 'Yes' response is indicative of respect, not necessarily indicative of complete agreement. You will hear this 'Yes' a lot more, whenever a superior assigns a task or says something. This response comes automatically, without even thinking whether a particular task can really be completed or not. You might think the team member has agreed to complete that work. However in reality, he is just responding that he heard you and is showing his respect by saying 'Yes'. This is a deep rooted cultural habit for Indians. In Indian family tradition, it is very important for younger people to respect elders. Whatever the elder says that needs to be followed without any questioning. All of us have been conditioned to do that. So, saying 'No' to a particular idea from an elder is seen as very disrespectful."

"I think I am able to follow you. But, I still don't see why saying 'Yes' is considered respect, saying 'No' is considered disrespectful," questioned John.

"There are two things a 'Yes' communicates. First one is that you are paying attention to what the elder is saying. Second, you are acknowledging that what the elder is saying makes sense. I remember, in my school days I was caned once for asking the teacher to explain again. He was furious that I asked him to repeat. He said 'What were you doing when I was teaching? If you pay proper attention, you will learn'. "

"Oh! I see. Now, I realize. I have noticed, few times in my sessions, the team members discussing among themselves. I stopped my presentation and asked if they needed any clarifications. But no one came forward with any questions. I assumed they understood everything. Thinking back, I feel they were not able to follow what I was explaining. Instead of asking me they were trying to get the clarifications from each other. Your explanation makes sense. How do we overcome this barrier?"

"It is simple. Don't accept a 'Yes' for any answer. Ask them to elaborate. Ask them to explain the concept or idea in their own words. If a person gets it wrong, make other team members to join in explaining it. Make it more interactive and participative. It will be an immediate feedback to you. I guess you did the same thing today."

"Yes, only then I realized there is something wrong. I will put these suggestions into practice."

"What suggestions? Can you elaborate?" asked Dheeraj mockingly.

John looked into Dheeraj's eyes, both had a hearty laugh. Both felt relieved.

Considering the relaxed atmosphere, Dheeraj continued, "John, even though this behavior seems to be a simple thing to handle, it has serious ramifications in the society. This behavior of saying 'Yes' is routed in the Indian family culture. Indian family is very hierarchical, where the head of the family has the complete authority, and others derive their authority based upon their position. The head of the family, a superior or a senior person has to decide what needs to be done and juniors have nothing but to implement. This phenomenon is deep rooted. It is reflected at homes, schools, work places and every other place. India is a hierarchical society. Children used to be punished if they opposed the elders; verbally and physically, at home and at school - it is changing now slowly. Because of this deep rooted cultural habit, Indians have this tendency of saying "yes" to everything said by an authority figure."

Dheeraj stopped and gulped some water. John could notice that Dheeraj had become very emotional.

Dheeraj cleared his throat and continued, "This behavior of submissiveness to an elder, the excessive interactions of Parent-to-Child are causing a lot of damage to India. Every institution is plagued by this one particular behavior. And it has led to rampant corruption and exploitation. Every authority figure, politicians, bureaucrats and God-men are able to exploit the people due to this conditioning. Recently, it has even affected one of the companies in our own Industry."

John, who was getting a little bored, became alert and curious on hearing the reference to IT industry.

"You might have heard about this news. One of the CEOs of Hyderabad based company got the dubious distinction of being on the list of Forbes 'World's 10 most outrageous CEOs'."

John nodded his head in affirmation.

"As the news goes, he had confessed to overstate its profits over several years and creating a fictitious cash balance of more than one billion dollars. I am sure; this could not have happened if anyone in the entire hierarchy questioned the anomalies they found. To top it all, he was surrounded by highly educated, respected and eminent people," said Dheeraj and paused for a while to check John's reaction.

"I feel this 'Yes' behavior made everyone in the hierarchy not to raise questions as well as not to suspect him of any wrong doing. This is the danger. A hierarchical society is as good as the chief. And you cannot expect every chief to be a good person. I would like to see our society encouraging democratic behavior at homes and schools. And I would like to see that happen very fast," said Dheeraj as if he was addressing a gathering.

He stood up and started staring into the sunset. John also stood up. Silently, they left the Canteen.

___***___

Good Work, Bad Work

It had been two weeks now. John slowed down his pace of explaining the Business Requirements. He followed the method suggested by Dheeraj in eliciting response from the team. He followed his presentation with a question & answer session, in which he asked the questions. He noticed that some of the team members were restless during the Q & A session. Nevertheless, John continued that practice and was happy that it worked so well. In those two weeks, he tried to encourage the team to be more open and share their views without any fear. He had been trying hard to develop the mutual trust and establish a democratic environment where team members could interact freely and fearlessly.

Nasreen was in his office to discuss the concerns that the team had expressed about two of the tasks - prototype development and documentation. Everyone in the team wanted to take part in the prototype development and no-one in the team was ready to take up documentation. Interestingly everyone in the team knew of the importance of documentation, but none was willing to take up that task. She tried to get that task assigned, but in vain. She came to John for help.

Just the previous day, John discussed about the next phase of the project with the team. He and Nasreen discussed in detail about the tasks involved and the assignments. They communicated the same to the team. John noticed some murmurs when the assignments were being announced. He felt it would be better to allow the team to decide about the allocation of work. So he left it to Nasreen to discuss with the team members and come to a consensus.

After listening to Nasreen, John commented, "Documentation is a very important task for any project. Without documentation, we cannot move forward. It is surprising, why no one wants to do it."

"I agree and everyone understands its importance. In fact, they themselves were victims of poor documentation in earlier projects. They also agree that the technical documents need to be prepared by themselves. But...," paused Nasreen.

John nodded his head to say to go ahead.

"But...they consider this task to be boring and menial."

"Menial?"

"Yes, they value the skill & experience of documentation as low. They value developing prototype very highly. They feel the experience of documentation lowers their value in the market. And on the other side, they feel prototype development experience increases the value."

"It's ridiculous. I agree documentation gets little boring compared to prototype development. But why should it lower one's value? Every task is equally important for us to complete the project successfully."

"Not only documentation, they categorize technologies also on the value scale. Everyone wants to jump on to the latest technology and gain experience in it. Just for the sake of experience, sometimes people come out with complex solutions to a simple problem. Anyway, it is better you decide the work assignments and announce them. They will follow," suggested Nasreen.

"Um. That is not the way I want. I want everyone to work wholeheartedly on the tasks they take up. I noticed, during our requirements' meeting, some of the team members paying little attention to the business terminology. I got a feeling that they don't value it also."

There was a moment of silence as both John and Nasreen were reflecting on this. John continued, "I am concerned. To provide a good solution, it is very important that we understand the problem. I will see Dheeraj about it. Thanks for updating me"

"Thanks," said Nasreen and left the room.

John stood up and went to see Dheeraj. He saw Dheeraj engrossed in perusing some notes.

John pretended a cough to get Dheeraj's attention and said, "Excuse me."

Dheeraj looked up and with a warm smile said, "Come in John." Noticing the look on John's face, he asked, "Is everything ok?"

"Yeah, I just wanted to discuss something. You seem to be busy, we can discuss later"

"I have 10 minutes for my meeting. Tell me briefly, what it is all about."

John explained about the tasks' assignment and his discussion with Nasreen. He wanted to know how to get the team's buy-in.

Dheeraj listened intently, "Yes. This is a major issue. People have this notion of high & low value work. And if it is not addressed properly, will lead to poor quality of work. How about we meet at our usual time?"

"That suits me. I will meet you at 4 PM."

※

"Right on time John! Come in," said Dheeraj after glancing at his watch.

"Have you ever had tea at those tea stalls?" asked Dheeraj, pointing out to the shanty places across the road.

John looked through the glass window. He could see a cluster of stalls- some covered by metal sheets and some with leaves similar to palm leaves. Many people were seen around them. He had been seeing them daily on his way-in and way-out of this building. He never thought about having tea at that place. He was curious to know what goes on there.

"No, I always had in our canteen only."

"Ok, let us go there today. You should visit these places. That is the best way to know India. I thought about the issue you talked about in the morning and decided to have our discussion out there."

"Ok. As long as you are there, I don't have any problem," said John, thinking of the people at those places. John realized that he had certain unknown fears about these people, and he had avoided interacting with this type of people at every place.

Both Dheeraj & John came out of their office, got down the elevator at the ground level. As they were leaving the building complex, John noticed the security guards saluting Dheeraj. He also noticed Dheeraj addressing them affectionately by their names and having a dialogue in their native language - Telugu.

That was the first-time John was walking along that path. The tea stalls were on the opposite side. They had to cross the road to go over there. The traffic was moderate. John looked around to find the zebra crossing and the walk signal. He looked towards Dheeraj, as he felt a tap on his shoulder.

"No Zebra crossings, no Walk signals at this place. We have to make our way through this traffic to the other side," said Dheeraj.

John looked at the traffic and felt there was no way to cross across safely. However to his surprise he noticed many people doing that with ease. They were moving from one lane to other, dodging the oncoming vehicles. The Frogger game - where a frog has to cross the road - came into his mind. Many a times he failed in making the frog avoid vehicles and cross it over to the other side. He also remembered what happens to the frog when it gets stuck on the road. Thinking about it a little shiver went down his spine.

Dheeraj noticed the look on John's face and smiled assuring him that everything would be fine.

"It appears scary, but in reality, it is not so. Everyone - the pedestrians, the vehicle drivers – understand each other. It is sort of a system that has its own mechanism of communication and trust in each other. Just grab my hand and flow with me." Without giving much time to John to ponder over his words, Dheeraj extended his left hand, which John grabbed firmly as if his life hanged at the end of it.

Dheeraj started crossing the road, waving to the drivers with his right hand and tugging at John to follow him. In few seconds, they were on the other side. John gave a sigh of relief, and all this appeared to him as marvel. He looked back at the traffic and amazed at how the pedestrians; the vehicles adjust themselves to allow for a smooth road crossing. Nevertheless, he felt that was an unnecessary adventure.

"Wow! Dheeraj, that was awesome. But why take this much risk, you should have Walk-signals."

"Yes, I agree. But that is how developing countries are, I guess. You see; we are surrounded by majestic buildings all around. Each one of them is self-sufficient and every amenity is provided for. One step out of them, you are faced with different environment. Many times I wonder why the same care is not extended to the common facilities such as these roads, by the people who built those buildings."

"Namaste sir," a man in a traditional white attire greeted Dheeraj, as they approached a tea stall.

"Namaste Ramaiah," said Dheeraj and enquired about him in Telugu. Dheeraj introduced Ramaiah to John as the owner of that stall.

That stall had around ten tables with four chairs around each of them. The chairs and the tables were made up of molded plastic. Dheeraj looked around and chose a table to sit. The man, Ramaiah, led them to the table, pulled out the chairs, dusted them off with a cloth for them to sit. John was feeling a little uncomfortable to sit as the chairs appeared dusty. The table also appeared a little unclean and there were two used cups and plates on it.

Ramaiah shouted aloud to call a person to pick up those used cups & plates. Dheeraj and John settled down in their chairs and waited for the cups & plates to be picked up. One man came running, looked at the table and he in turn shouted aloud to call another person. John was wondering at the goings-on. He understood that those two men wanted to get those cups & plates picked up; however unable to understand why they were not doing so. Both the men were looking around and yelling for someone. It took few minutes before a boy arrived with a plastic tub and picked up those cups & plates and dumped them into his tub. During all this time, Ramaiah was apologizing to Dheeraj and was assuring that the table will be set in no time. Ramaiah asked the second man to take the order from Dheeraj, and with a bow took leave from both. Dheeraj ordered for two teas. The man in turn shouted aloud "TWO SPECIAL TEA" to someone inside.

"Instant wireless communication," said Dheeraj to explain what was happening. "By the way, what were we discussing?"

"Walk-Signals"

"Oh! Yeah. I guess there might be issues with the civic authorities on the common facilities, but I feel they can all be overcome if there is a will among all these builders to address those issues."

Dheeraj stopped for a while, as a boy bent over the table and wiped it clean with a towel, and then continued. "Even where we have full control of the common facilities, the people are not willing to come forward. I think I should not be telling you this, but Indians' community orientation needs lots of improvements."

"I see, don't you learn about Community work at school?"

"No. That is lacking. And you are right! Schools are the best places to cultivate habits and to bring about cultural change."

Dheeraj paused to take money out of his wallet and gave it to the waiter who placed the teacups on the table. John looked at the waiter and said, "Thanks."

Both started sipping the tea.

"Hmmm…the smell is good and tasty too," commented John. He was enjoying the open air. As he was observing the surroundings, he saw a person fixing the roof; hammering and throwing the pieces to the ground. The place was vibrant with people discussing & arguing animatedly, and sometimes it appeared to him as if they were going to fight. He noticed that there was lot of physical contact among people here. Earlier, he mistook those interactions to be violent. Now, watching the people from close proximity in the secure company of Dheeraj, a new perspective was dawning on him.

"By the way, you wanted to discuss something about the work assignments, right?" asked Dheeraj.

"Yes, today morning Nasreen told me that no one in the team is interested in taking up the documentation work. Not only that, she told me they consider it as a menial task. That surprised me. I don't want to push people to do a task. I want their buy-in."

"I understand your perspective," said Dheeraj sympathetically.

"This is the next phase of the project. I thought I should discuss with you right away, so that I don't slip on my timelines," said John.

"I understand the problem. To some extent, the team members' disinterest in documentation is justified. They want to have all high-tech stuff on their resumes. I guess this is rooted in the perception that documentation experience does not bolster their resume value. So there is less value attached to it. The concept of treating every task within a project as equally important has not yet fully imbibed. Many a times, the team is not focused on the overall goal of the project. They don't see the big picture. To phrase it another way, they miss the forest for the trees. They are interested in the individual task and …." The conversation stopped as they heard a commotion.

Ramaiah was arguing with the roof repairer loudly. The roof repairer had his bag of tools over his shoulder and appeared ready to leave the place. Ramaiah was pointing to the debris the roof repairer has thrown around and yelling at him. John asked Dheeraj what was going on.

"Ramaiah hired that guy to fix the roof. He did fix the roof. While fixing it, he has thrown the broken pieces around. Ramaiah wants him to clean the place and leave. But the roof repairer is refusing to do that. He says his job is to fix the roof and not to clean the place of the debris out of it. It is a classic example for the discussion we are having."

"Hmmmmmm......you know what? When we came here, this Ramaiah did not pick up the empty cups & plates from our table. Even the next guy did not pick up. We had to wait until a 3rd guy came and picked them up. All the while, these two guys were standing and watching. It is funny, now he is asking that guy to clean up the mess," said John shrugging his shoulders.

"It appears you are seeing the pattern, John. I am not sure whether you have heard about the Caste system in India."

"Yes, I did read about it. If I remember correctly, it says the Indian society is divided into four or five groups called castes. The basis of this division is the skills or professions they practice."

"You are right. The biggest problem is that they have a hierarchy. They are ranked. So you have high castes and low castes. Interestingly enough, there are further sub-castes in each of these groups, and they are also ranked within that group. This concept is ingrained in our society. That is reflected automatically in looking at a job as high value and low value."

"Does the caste play a role in how you hire people for your company?"

"No, not at all. In the workplace, the caste has almost vanished. But once you step outside of the office, it is still there. Now the hierarchy works differently; the caste aspect is being displaced by the power and social status you have. Even though we have democracy as our political system, it has not impacted the hierarchical society. So, even now a person as well as a job is measured in terms of its status or rank."

"I get it," said John, with his face lit up with excitement. "The roof repairer considers the cleaning up the mess he created, as demeaning. Ramaiah considers picking up the empty cups & plates is for a low-ranking person. Similarly, my team members consider documentation as menial."

"You are connecting the dots very fast. The challenge is to break this mindset. Somehow, we have to make people embrace the dignity of labor."

"May be we should start with the issue I am facing," said John to get the focus back on to his immediate problem.

"Yeah. Now that you got some perspective about the good work & bad work, how do you want to proceed?" asked Dheeraj.

"First, I would convey in all possible means that every task is important. I will also convey that I value all team members and their work equally. I might come to you to address the team, if required."

"No problem, John. I am available always," assured Dheeraj.

"I can think of two options to communicate that I value everyone equally. One of the options is to break-down the documentation work further and to assign everyone a piece of that task. The other option is to assign everyone a module and ask them to take care of everything for that. On the prototype development, I will have brainstorming sessions where everyone gets a chance to contribute ideas. The development will be done by few, but at-least I will give everyone an opportunity to participate," said John.

"Excellent! John. You are on the right track. The exact implementation might change depending upon the circumstances. Sometimes you might have to use your veto power. As long as you understand the underlying phenomenon for a particular behavior and try to address that, you are fine," encouraged Dheeraj.

"Thanks Dheeraj. By the way, you seem to have very good relationship with Ramaiah. I am sure you would have given a lot of advice and lectures to him. How is that he did not get the idea of dignity of labor?" asked John. "I am referring to the picking up of used cups & plates."

"I failed there. It is not easy to break the culturally deep-rooted habits. We will succeed more with young children. As you have pointed out earlier, the best way to bring about cultural transformation is through schools," said Dheeraj.

"Are you done with your tea?" asked Dheeraj. John nodded affirmatively.

"Let me demonstrate you something," said Dheeraj standing up. John got the cue to leave the place, and followed.

Dheeraj looked around and found Ramaiah sitting behind the cash counter. He waved to Ramaiah to say good-bye. Ramaiah stood up and folded his hands to say Namaste. John was wondering about the demonstration Dheeraj referred to. Dheeraj picked up the two cups from the table in his left hand and held them up in the view of Ramaiah. With his right hand, he waved good-bye again. Dheeraj pushed back his chair and casually moved towards the tub where all used utensils are put.

All of a sudden, Ramaiah started walking briskly towards Dheeraj. He grabbed the cups from Dheeraj and mumbled few words. Dheeraj patted on the back of Ramaiah with affection, and both Dheeraj & John left the place. John could not understand all that happened now. This same Ramaiah did not touch the cups when they walked in. Now, he almost did a sprint to get to Dheeraj and took them from Dheeraj.

Dheeraj noticed the puzzled face of John and asked, "How is the demonstration?"

"I am confused," replied John.

"Nothing to get confused, it is the same rank system working here. Ramaiah respects me. He considers me to be a rank higher than him. In a hierarchical system, the person who is at a lower rank should take care of the higher rank person. So he came to my rescue," said Dheeraj smilingly. John nodded his head in satisfaction.

Both of them crossed the road to get to the office. John was more comfortable this time.

As soon as they entered the office, John went straight to Nasreen's cubicle. Nasreen was still working on the computer.

"Hi Nasreen, what! You are still around!" said John looking at his watch.

"I have something to complete and decided to stay back. How did your meeting go with Dheeraj?"

"It was great. Today we went to the tea stall outside for our discussion," said John and explained all that happened there.

"It is interesting to know. I never interpreted things this way," commented Nasreen. "I guess when we take a step out of the system and see, we get a new perspective. Your presence seems to be helping in that."

"It never occurred to me how much influence culture has on the way we work," said John.

"About good work and bad work, let me tell you another aspect in our culture," said Nasreen. "In our homes, our parents treat the boys and girls differently. Many of the tasks are clearly marked as boys' tasks and girls' tasks."

"For example, girls are supposed to do cooking, setting up the dining table, do the dishes and keep the house clean. Boys consider this work as bad work. They forget that if those tasks are not done, they won't have food. See they don't realize how important those tasks are and how good that work is," concluded Nasreen with heavy gestures.

John was amused to see Nasreen gestures. He thanked her for bringing the issue to his attention and left the place saying, "See you tomorrow, Nasreen."

---***---

Life Skills, Party and Documentation

John turned around to see as he heard a familiar voice. It was Dheeraj standing just behind him in the lunch-line and was talking with another person.

"Hi Dheeraj," said John.

"Hi John," replied Dheeraj.

"This is the first time I met you during the lunch time," commented John.

"Yeah, today I am early for my lunch. I have a meeting to attend immediately after my lunch. By the way, this is Anup," Dheeraj introduced the other person to John. "Anup, this is John." Anup and John shook hands.

"John, I looked at your project reports. Congratulations! You are ahead of your schedule," said Dheeraj.

"Thanks. I did not expect this progress. The team is very good. They are committed and hard working," said John.

"Glad to know that. Let us have a party then. How about going out for dinner this Friday with the entire team?" asked Dheeraj.

"Yeah! That is a great idea. Let me check with the team and confirm," replied John.

"Ok" said Dheeraj and motioned John to move on, as the people standing in front of John moved ahead. John picked up a plate and filled it with Roti (Indian bread), noodles, chicken curry and some green salad. Dheeraj followed him and filled his plate with Roti, Rice, Chicken curry and salad. Both waited for Anup to pick up his lunch.

Dheeraj looked around to choose a table for their lunch. A couple of people waved at Dheeraj asking him to join them. He nodded his head to all of them in acknowledgement. Pointing to a table which was occupied by a lone person, Dheeraj said, "Let us join him."

John looked at that person. He saw him earlier a few times. He must be in his 50s, well-built and respectable. As they approached his table, he looked at Dheeraj with a radiant smile. Dheeraj put his plate on the table and moved towards him saying, "Namaste *Anna*, It has been a long time since we met." The gentleman put down his spoon & fork and stood up to give a warm hug to Dheeraj and patted Dheeraj's back with affection. All of them exchanged greetings and settled down for their lunch.

Dheeraj turned to John and said, "Meet Prakash garu; He is our Quality & Training head. He is like my elder brother. In management terms, he is my mentor and guide."

John greeted Prakash.

"*Anna,* this is John, Project Manager from USA," said Dheeraj

"Oh! I see. Nice meeting you John. I have never seen you before. When did you come?" asked Prakash.

"Oh! It is almost three months now. I know you. I have sent my project's Quality reports to your team," replied John and briefly explained about his project.

"Yeah! I have seen your project's Quality reports. You seem to be making good progress, John. Keep it up," said Prakash.

"Thanks. It is all my team's effort and Dheeraj's guidance. Maybe, I should start calling Dheeraj '*Anna*'," said John mockingly. Everyone laughed on hearing the way John said *Anna.*

"Whether we call him '*Anna*' or not, Dheeraj is readily available for all of us to guide," said Anup. "He is the mentor for many of us in this location."

"We enjoy his discussions and his perspectives on every subject," said Prakash. "Hope, you are not getting tortured by his lectures," enquired Prakash from John, while looking at Dheeraj teasingly.

"Not at all! On the other hand, it benefited me a lot in understanding my team members. It directly helped me in managing this project. Part of the success so far is due to that. Now, I know little more about the Indian culture and its relation to work," said John.

"That is interesting. How come he has not yet taught you how to eat a Roti?" said Prakash smilingly. John stopped biting the Roti and looked at others to see how everyone else is eating. Dheeraj, Anup and Prakash were tearing the Roti with both hands. They folded the piece of Roti into a scoop, with that picked up the curry and ate it. He observed himself, he was holding the Roti in his left hand and taking a bite of the Roti; and was scooping a little curry with a spoon in his right hand and putting into his mouth.

Noticing that John figured out the difference, Prakash continued "You will get the best taste when you eat the way we do. You should try it once."

"Sure. I noticed some of the people here eating rice also with their bare hand. I mean without using spoon or fork," said John.

"I also eat my food – rice & Roti - with my bare hand at home. It gives me complete satisfaction" said Dheeraj. "As you know, our food consists of mainly rice & Roti, with lots of curries in the liquid & semi-liquid form. You will get the best flavor and best taste when you mix the curry well in your rice. That, you can do only with your bare hand. However, at office and other places, I use the spoon to mix the curry with rice and eat," explained Dheeraj.

"Chinese also eat rice. But they use Chopsticks to eat," commented Anup.

"That is true. I don't really know what they have in place of our curries. But how come we Indians did not invent a tool for eating so far?" wondered Dheeraj.

"I feel the usage of tools is not our forte," said Prakash. "For example, if you look at bathing, many countries used some sort of a bath tub and a brush for rubbing one's back. In India, we won't find any traces of them. One should read the book 'Discovery of India' by Jawaharlal Nehru. At one point, he mentions about how Indians are not good at appreciating tools' usage and missed the Industrial revolution. He specifically points about the disinterest of Indians in printing technology."

"You are right. There seems to be an inherent dislike for tools usage in our culture," said Dheeraj and continued. "In my previous company, we had contract-workers to mop the floor throughout the day. All the workers were ladies. They used to crouch on the floor and mop it with a cloth. It was so demeaning. I suggested to the admin guy to put a rule that the mopping should be done standing with appropriate tools. But, it never got implemented. Many people, I think, consider tools as support systems for handicapped only."

"Even wearing safety gadgets is also considered in the same way," added Anup. "My son resists wearing the helmet while riding his bike. The main reason is that the other children heckling at him for wearing a helmet. Similarly, many people despise putting on the seat belts in cars."

"There is a sort of heroism attached to doing things with bare hands, I presume. If you notice, as per our climatic conditions, we should all be wearing hats and sunglasses. But wearing them is considered as stylish rather than a necessity." Before Prakash could say the next thing, Dheeraj added, "I think, protecting oneself with headgear is still practiced in rural areas and typically by lower-middle-class people. They tie a long clothe as 'Pagdi' – a sort of headgear; and in North India, people wear Gandhi caps. Somehow the middle-class and rich people abandoned that practice."

"That is a good observation, Dheeraj," said Prakash. "By the way, we have noticed a similar attitude towards using tools for our work," said Prakash. Looking at John, he continued, "Hope you are able to see your team using the tools more, especially debugger. We have initiated many training programs on the various tools of our trade, including Word, Excel and MS-Project."

"Yeah, I attended the MS-Project training program on the advice of Dheeraj," said John. "I have used it before, but the training has unfolded many other features I never thought that existed. It is a good idea that everyone should attend a training program before he uses a tool. It will help them understand what is possible. And also exposes them to all the features available in it. Otherwise, we tend to use the basic features only."

"Training paves the way for Quality. The Quality of a person, an organization or a society is dependent on the extent, content and vigor of training they receive. Dheeraj, did you notice how many different ways people eat, using their hands? " asked Prakash.

All of them looked around. They noticed many people using spoons & forks and few using their bare hands to eat. John felt that the way people were using spoons & forks differed from one person to other. And as far as the people who were eating rice with bare hands, they appeared to be eating in the same way.

"You might have noticed that usage of the fork & spoon is not the same with everyone," commented Prakash.

Everyone nodded their heads. Before Prakash could continue, Dheeraj said, "There are differences too in the way people are eating the rice with bare hands." Prakash gave an admiring glance and signaled Dheeraj to continue. "The differences are due to the family backgrounds. We learn how to eat with bare hands from our parents. And as we all know there are huge differences among the family traditions. As far as usage of spoon & fork is concerned, we were never trained. Most of us learnt on our own."

"Excellent observation, Dheeraj!" said Prakash. "In our family, there is a rule. When you eat with your bare hands, food should not touch your palm. You have to use your fingers dexterously to mix the food and eat. As you have rightly pointed out, each family continues the habits, traditions they learn through generations. Unfortunately, these are not taught in our schools."

"Wow! Great explanation," said Anup looking at his right hand.

"We should teach these skills – I call them Life Skills – at primary school," said Prakash. "We should train every child how to eat, how to maintain hygiene, how to brush & bathe, how to keep the house and surroundings clean. We should also teach other things that make them ready for life outside the school -how to follow the traffic signals; how to travel in a bus, train, airplane; how to operate a bank account; how to use a phone; how to contact police and file a complaint; how to contact emergency services, etc."

"But, in Government primary schools, more than 50% of the children are poor," said Anup. "They may not even be having proper meals every day. What is the point in telling about all of these?"

"That is the very reason we should train them in all these," replied Prakash. "See Anup, some of us are lucky that we are born in well-to-do families. So, we get better exposure. What about the children from other families?" asked Prakash. "We should make every child experience them at least vicariously. We should show them videos. We should make them role play. We should make them do some projects. They in turn will carry that knowledge back to their homes."

"I agree," said Dheeraj. "For example, a child learning about Post-office or bank can help his parents open an account there. It is a great idea. Primary school students are the knowledge channels to every home," commented Dheeraj.

John was enjoying all this conversation. In these three months, he observed the many unique cultural aspects of India. Even though he could not understand the history or the reasons underlying some aspects; he started appreciating most of them. Once in a while he tried to emulate, but not very successfully. He was thinking about the tools' usage by his team. He was wondering whether he could attribute the significant progress of the project solely to the hard work put in by the team. He was curious how much of it is due to the tools' usage. He decided to check with the team. His thoughts got interrupted by Dheeraj asking, "Are we done?" - referring to the lunch. Everyone nodded in affirmative.

"Ok, *Anna*! See you later," said Dheeraj as he got up. All of them picked up their plates and cups to leave them at the counter. As they were walking towards the counter, John said to Dheeraj, "Nasreen told me that you guys won't pick up the plates at home. But here…."

"Yeah that is true. We have put this rule here in the company. So everyone got this habit. However, once they are back in homes, many of them won't do this there and expect the women to pick them up. One of the justifications earlier was that women were full-time homemakers," said Dheeraj.

"I enjoyed having lunch with you all. Now, I know why many people were inviting you to join their table. It was great fun. I should join you for lunch more often," said John.

"Oh! Thanks. By the way, we are going to have dinner with the team this Friday. Right?" asked Dheeraj, while placing the plate & cup on the conveyor belt.

"Sure. I will get back to you with the confirmation," said John as they both walked out of the Canteen.

CR80

Friday 6:50 PM. Dheeraj just got into the shopping complex. He went straight to the elevator to go to the restaurant on 7th floor. At the elevator, he was greeted by John, Nasreen and two other members. They were the only people waiting at the elevator. As they were exchanging greetings, the elevator door opened. Before they could get in, four other people came rushing and forced themselves into the elevator. John looked at Dheeraj with a perplexed face. Now, there is space for three more people only. So John & Dheeraj decided to stay back and asked others to take the elevator.

"Looks like we have a training issue here," commented John smilingly.

"Yep, that is one factor. There is another factor – Scarcity Mentality. People are afraid that the elevator may not function later, say due to power cut, elevator failure, etc." said Dheeraj.

"Yeah, I was told that there are some scheduled power cuts. Doesn't this building have generators?" asked John.

"Yes, it does. We won't be facing any problem," assured Dheeraj. "But, being a country of billion people, the resources are always in shortage. People do face problems if they miss an opportunity. I am not justifying the behavior, just giving another perspective," said Dheeraj.

Few other people joined them in waiting. This time, when the elevator door opened, others waited till Dheeraj & John got into it. John was wondering, whether they heard their conversation.

The elevator reached the 7th floor. As the door opened, John could see the main entrance to the restaurant. A well-dressed usher bowed to them and escorted them into the restaurant. John looked around and was fascinated by the decoration. It appeared like a movie setting. The theme appeared to be an Indian village setting, with the staff dressed in traditional village attire. The background music was melodious. "It is an old Hindi song," said Dheeraj as if he read John's mind.

Dheeraj noticed Nasreen and others sitting around a table and moved towards them. As they approached them, some of them started getting up as a mark of respect to Dheeraj. Dheeraj motioned at them to sit down, and both John & Dheeraj took their seats.

"Good to see you all on time," commented Dheeraj. He looked around to see if everyone of the team is present. "Where is Sanjay?" asked Dheeraj noticing his absence.

"He is still in the office. He called me and informed that he would be joining us late," replied Nasreen.

"Working so late on a party day!" exclaimed Dheeraj.

"He is building a Release. He is our release in-charge. Once he starts the process, it takes two full days for him to complete a Build & Release," said Nasreen.

"Yes. That is true," said John. "He is a very hard-working guy. He does not want to take anyone's help too. He is the only guy who knows this process of Build & Release. As you know, it is a critical process and any mix up will cause a problem. So every time we make a release of new version, he works very diligently and puts in 15 to 18 hours a day, for 2 to 3 days continuously. I greatly appreciate his commitment and expertise."

Dheeraj wondered why it should take so long and why this guy had to work alone. He asked, "How often you make a new release of your application."

"Every four weeks," replied John.

"It is good to know that Sanjay is putting that much effort every month. But, John, I think you should find out how you can provide help to him," said Dheeraj. Dheeraj noticed murmuring among the team members. He decided to talk about it next day with John.

"Are you ready for the order, Sir?" asked the waiter.

With that question, everyone focused their attention on the menu and got involved in animated discussion about what to order. After a couple of minutes everyone placed their orders. One of them called up Sanjay to know his preferences and gave out his order too.

While they were waiting for their drinks & appetizers, they discussed movies and joked about each other. John was enjoying the teasing among the team members. He observed that they had no inhibitions about each other. The female team members were reserved in their behavior, but the men were showing lot of camaraderie and a lot of bonhomie among them. He wondered how they can become so close to each other. The same noisy, loud discussions continued throughout the party.

Everyone had a great time at the party. Sanjay, the hardworking Build & Release in-charge, joined them when the desserts were being served. John gave special attention to him so as to express his appreciation for his extraordinary efforts. Dheeraj mingled with them freely and encouraged discussions about movies, friends and social life. At the end, Dheeraj congratulated John & the team for their great work.

CB80

The next day, Dheeraj stopped by John's room and said, "Good Morning John, hope you had good sleep yesterday."

"Good Morning. Yep! But I am yet to come out of the party mood. Thanks for joining us yesterday," replied John.

"No problem. I enjoy spending time with the teams. It motivates the team and gives me firsthand information about how the team is working," said Dheeraj. After a brief pause, he asked, "By the way, what do you think about Sanjay's work?"

"Oh! He is a great guy. I have not seen a person working so hard. He is very committed. See, last night when everyone was partying he was working alone. He handles the Build & Release work single handedly, without taking anyone's help," replied John.

"That is great. But, I feel sorry for him. I think we should provide help to him so that he could complete the work during the work hours, and say not to miss parties. Did you find out why the Build & Release process takes 2 to 3 days?" enquired Dheeraj.

"Yeah! I asked him a couple of times. It seems there are many tasks that need to be done in a sequence. He does not want to take chances with others as he is afraid a single mistake will lead to re-doing the whole process again," replied John.

"I see. Is this process documented?" asked Dheeraj.

"Yes, in a way. Sanjay has handwritten notes. For some reason or other, he postpones preparing a formal document. He justifies saying, 'any way I am the person to do this, I have my notes to refer.' And he is able to complete this task every time satisfactorily" explained John.

"Satisfactorily!" exclaimed Dheeraj.

"Yes, we don't get a perfect release. We have to do little tweaking after the release, to make that version work," said John.

"John, we have an opportunity here to improve the process of Build & Release," said Dheeraj. "This task is a very good candidate for documentation. It is a task that needs to be done repeatedly; it has lot of steps to complete, and a misstep will lead to re-doing the whole work. You should ask him to convert his handwritten notes into an electronic document say Word document or an Excel document. While Sanjay is watching over, let someone else do the Build & Release on a test system following the instructions mentioned in that document."

Dheeraj continued, "Don't expect everything to go right on the first try. They might have to repeat the process to identify and note down every step required to complete the process successfully. As our Quality guru Prakash says 'Say what you do and do what you say.' It means 'Document how you Do and Do as per the Document.' That way you will have a standard process. If someone finds a better way of doing the same task, the document can be updated so that everyone follows the improved process."

"I guess documenting a process is the first step for improving the Quality," reflected John.

"Absolutely!" said Dheeraj appreciatively as he was happy that John understood what he meant. "Documenting a process helps you review the document and see if there are any tasks that can be done in parallel. You can help Sanjay review the process, and I bet there will be opportunities for parallel tasks. With that you can provide another resource to help Sanjay complete the task in shorter duration. The other benefit is you will have other resources to do the same task. So in a situation where Sanjay is not available you won't be helpless."

"I get it. We did have that problem once. I had to postpone the release by a week when Sanjay was not well. But, Dheeraj, I tried a couple of times to get this process documented, but did not get a positive response from Sanjay. For some reason, he is reluctant to create a document." said John with a concern.

"I noticed that reluctance with many people. One of the main reasons is that documenting a process makes that knowledge known to everyone. Many people get power by withholding the knowledge. Documenting makes people lose that exclusive power of knowledge. Some people feel vulnerable about their jobs. They fear that by sharing the knowledge they make themselves available for replacement by others. So, it is your responsibility to drive away that fear," explained Dheeraj.

"Wow! I never thought so deep about it. Thanks Dheeraj for explaining all this. I will try my best to communicate to the team that everyone's job is secured. Hmmm……I remember now, few people expressed their intention to learn this Build & Release process and volunteered to help Sanjay. But, he always refused," said John.

"I know. That is the typical behavior of an insecure person. There is an underlying cultural factor too for this," continued Dheeraj.

"Ok!" said John smilingly. "I was waiting for that point of view."

"We will have that discussion some other day, John. It is about 'Competition versus Cooperation'," said Dheeraj. "For now, best wishes with documentation. Get in touch with me if you need any help in getting the process documented or reviewed," volunteered Dheeraj warmly and left the room.

---***---

Competition Vs Cooperation

It was the time of the year; Dheeraj had trouble making a decision. He was a bit early in the office that day. He pulled the venetian blinds fully up and was looking outside through the glass. The early morning sun was warming up the eastern skies. The road was getting busier with the traffic. The workers of Ramaiah's canteen were cleaning and arranging the chairs & tables. He could see Ramaiah bellow his instructions to his workers. Dheeraj's attention was drawn to the garbage bin a little away from Ramaiah's canteen. There were a few stray dogs fighting over the food left in the garbage bin. Dheeraj could feel the vicious barking of the dogs, even though he could not hear it. One fierce dog took over the bin by barking-out at others. In that fight, some food fell outside the bin. The rest of the dogs fought over that and one of them took full possession of it. His eyes caught the glimpse of the Scorpio near the gate. That was John's vehicle. It brought Dheeraj's attention back to the problem at hand.

He moved away from the window and occupied his chair looking at the paper on his table. It was a list of names. These were provided by his team leads. These were the people whom their leaders considered as the 'best employees' in their team. It had Sanjay's name suggested by John. Now, Dheeraj had to pick ONE from this list and provide it to Vinod Mehta for consideration for the 'Best Employee of The Year' award. These awards were to be given in the forthcoming company's Annual day function. He faced the same situation last year. As it was 1st Annual day function for him, he forced himself to choose one and rationalized his selection. This time, he was not able to do the same.

Dheeraj had strong views about singling out a person for outstanding performance. The mechanism of selection was not very objective and prone to biases. He felt it alienates the rest of the people and builds unhealthy competition. Instead, he felt there should be an award for the 'Best Project Team'. This could be done objectively based on the project metrics. Within that team, the team could vote to select a person as the 'Best Team Member'.

He got up from his chair and started strolling down the aisle in front of his room. He was in conflict and thinking deeply about how to resolve. His thoughts got interrupted by a friendly voice "Good Morning Dheeraj! What is going on?"

It was Prakash. Dheeraj just realized that he walked into Prakash's room. "Sit down. What is that you are thinking so deeply? Anything I can help you with?" prodded Prakash. This was nothing new for Prakash. Dheeraj had the liberty of barging into Prakash's room whenever his mind is cluttered with ideas. Prakash was all game for playing the role of a 'sounding board'.

"Good Morning *Anna*!" replied Dheeraj. "Yes, I have an issue that is bothering me. I want to check it with you. Do you have few minutes?" asked Dheeraj settling down in the chair.

Prakash was well aware that it was something very important. "Absolutely! Go ahead," encouraged Prakash while leaning forward.

"For the Annual day awards, I was asked to choose 'Best Employee' from my group," said Dheeraj getting straight to the topic. "I am against the idea of singling out one person as the best employee," said Dheeraj and explained his views about awarding 'Best Team' award in place of 'Best Employee' at company level and 'Best Team Member' at the team level.

Prakash listened attentively and commented, "Even in your scheme, you are singling out one person as the best team player in a team. How is it different?"

"It is done at a team level, where everyone has direct interactions with that person. And the person is chosen by the vote. It is not done across the teams. Comparing a best team member from one team to another team will not be objective and is not right. How a person contributes to a team depends on the team's situation," explained Dheeraj.

"So you object to the idea of managers nominating a person," asked Prakash.

"Yes! In a way. This type of award encourages competitiveness at the expense of cooperation. We should instill cooperation and team spirit in every person to achieve greater results. This is akin to the rankings that are given in schools. Due to that we see unhealthy competition to stay at the top by causing a downfall of others. People even refer to it as cut-throat-competition," said Dheeraj and took a deep breath.

"I have personal experiences of parents getting overly concerned about the rankings. Hope you remember the incident I narrated to you last year. When my son got the 1st rank in the Quarterly exams of 4th grade, I was visited by two policemen….."

Before Dheeraj could complete, Prakash said, "…..Yeah! A police officer's wife 'summoned' you to their house to know how your son could get the 1st rank by pushing her daughter to 2nd rank."

"Yes. It was a shock to her to see her daughter lose the 1st rank. She created a big scene in the school and talked to my wife over the phone to get the subject-wise marks, etc. Her daughter was the 1st ranker all through the 1st grade to 3rd grade. She could not bear the news of her daughter losing the rank in 4th grade."

"That too, to a newly joined kid who just returned from America," added Prakash.

"Exactly!" said Dheeraj. "I see this behavior of one-upmanship among our team members also. I have seen people becoming very possessive about their knowledge and going to great extents to avoid sharing it. The other day John pointed out the difficulty in getting one of his team members, Sanjay, document his process. This is a classic example of possessiveness and unwillingness to share one's knowledge. By the way, you know whom John has nominated for 'Best Employee'?"

"Who?" countered Prakash.

"Sanjay!" replied Dheeraj. "Sanjay is the only one who does the Build & Release in that team. He does it single handedly, refusing help from others. And he works for long hours continuously for 2 to 3 days to complete the task. So.......John has his reasons to nominate him as the 'Best Employee'."

"I see what you are driving at. By not documenting and by not sharing, Sanjay might be contributing negatively to the team. It is possible others may not consider him as a good team player too," reflected Prakash.

"You said it! It is very important that as leaders, we encourage the right behavior. Many a times, we end up doing the quite opposite, and don't even realize that we are to be blamed for the situation. I instructed all team-leads to reward teamwork and accept every team member as-is," said Dheeraj.

"What do you mean by as-is?" asked Prakash.

"What I mean is to accept every team member for their strengths, attitude and teamwork; and not to focus only on their individual contribution. In a team, we end up having people with different strengths and weaknesses. It is for the leader to recognize them and put them to the best use for the common goal of the team. What is important is to see how each of them is improving themselves and contributing to the team's goals," continued Dheeraj. "So, during the performance appraisal each individual should be measured against that individual's past performance. The top rating should be given to the individual who contributes to the team significantly, apart from meeting his own targets."

"I agree. But, what do you want to do now?" asked Prakash, bringing back the focus to the issue on hand.

"You suggest. I feel we need to have a discussion with top management on this," replied Dheeraj.

"Ok. Let us meet Vinod and you can share your views with him. I will check with him and setup a meeting," assured Prakash.

"That will be great. You also think about it and we can have a good discussion with Vinod on this," said Dheeraj standing up.

ೞ೮

Few minutes back, Prakash called Dheeraj to inform about the meeting with Vinod. Vinod agreed to meet them the next day at 11:00 AM. Dheeraj was excited about the opportunity to share his views with the location head. The thought of 'Best Employee' and Sanjay came to his mind. He was wondering how Sanjay was handling the documentation efforts. It was three days ago he had the discussion with John. He decided to check with John. He looked at his watch and walked towards the canteen to catch John there.

Luckily for him, he found John & Nasreen having tea in the canteen. He picked up a cup of tea and joined them. Both John & Nasreen were happy to see Dheeraj joining them. After exchange of pleasantries, Dheeraj asked John about the documentation efforts.

"We made good progress. It was good that you have pointed that out" said John. "It took considerable effort to make Sanjay agree for this. He could only agree when I & Nasreen sat with him to go through the entire process. Nasreen prepared the documentation while he was explaining the process."

"Good. Did you find any opportunities for improvement?" asked Dheeraj.

"Yes, we did review and found few steps that can be carried out simultaneously. There are few things each developer has to take care, so that the entire Build & Release process can be reduced to one day!" explained Nasreeen.

"We are still in the process of getting all the steps right. I am sure we can automate certain steps to reduce the entire time to few hours," said John confidently.

"Excellent! Way to go! Good job guys!" commented Dheeraj.

"By the way, entire team knows about this documentation effort. A couple of them are interested in taking up this work. I think, once we verify and get all the steps right, anyone from the team can complete this work," said John proudly. He turned towards Nasreen and asked, "What do you say Nasreen?"

Nasreen nodded affirmatively and said, "Sanjay appeared hurt. All this while, he did not allow anyone to look at what he was doing. He is the only one with this knowledge. Now he feels that he has lost the power of this exclusive knowledge."

"He deserves credit for having gained this knowledge. We should acknowledge that" said Dheeraj. Addressing John, Dheeraj continued, "You should find out if he has any job insecurity feelings. Many a times, I have seen insecure people not willing to share the knowledge. As a leader it is our responsibility to dispel that fear of job insecurity. We should treat every team member with equal respect irrespective of their caliber. Once we have accepted a person as a team member, we should try to get the best out of him and provide opportunities for his growth. It is very important to encourage people to share and contribute to the team's development."

"But sir!" said Nasreen hesitantly. "To get recognition from the management, many people try to outdo others just like we used to do in schools. I know many guys trying to outperform others. They all are very competitive and want to retain their edge. I guess it provides job security also."

"I don't see anything wrong with competitiveness," exclaimed John.

"Competitiveness in itself is not bad. A healthy competition is good for everybody," said Dheeraj and continued. "If a person competes against his own performance, it is a very good sign. It would lead to greater improvement in his performance. Many times this competition is not against his performance; it is in comparison with the others, i.e. in terms of ranks. If somebody wants to look better, look successful he has to just compare with others who have not done well; and if he has done a little better, he will be seen as a successful person. Unfortunately, this idea of one-upmanship will come in the way of achieving team's goals and brings down individual's productivity too. John, do you remember the traffic jam on your first day in Hyderabad?" asked Dheeraj.

John recollected the scene of his first day. They were stuck in a traffic jam at a crossroad. The traffic red lights were flashing. There was utter chaos. Everyone wanted to be the first person to be out of that traffic jam. In that process everyone was blocking the way of every other person, and no one could move an inch. Entire traffic came to a standstill.

"Yeah!" said John excitedly. "Wow! I had never been in a situation like that. It was like American football. All vehicles were almost touching each other physically and pushing their way through it. I am not sure, how long we got stuck up; it felt like eternity for me. No one got benefited by that. Everyone ended up being there for long time. If they followed a pattern of letting each other go, the way we do at 'all-way STOP' signs, everyone would be assured of moving out of it at a certain time. My God! It was such a scene! Somehow you & Venkat managed to get us out of that."

"What is the 'all-way STOP' sign?" enquired Nasreen.

"Hey! Don't you know what an 'all-way STOP' sign is? You told me you ride a two-wheeler too!" teased John.

"I am not kidding John," said Nasreen and turning towards Dheeraj, she asked, "What is he referring to?"

"He is referring to the 'STOP' signs erected at road junctions. You must make a complete stop behind the stop-line and wait for a safe gap in the traffic before you move off. It is very interesting to see the traffic flow at 'all-way STOP." After a complete stop has been made, the first vehicle to arrive at the intersection gets the right-of-way to proceed. Every driver will make a mental note of the order in which they arrived at the junction. And everyone waits for his turn patiently," explained Dheeraj. Looking at the confused face of Nasreen, Dheeraj turned to John and said, "John, you should show a traffic video on YouTube to Nasreen. This traffic sign is not known to many."

"Wow! No wonder we had that traffic jam. When the red lights flash, it is considered as 'all-way STOP'. I wonder how you've been riding your two-wheeler, Nasreen!" said John. Nasreen gave a stern look at John and shrugged her shoulders.

"The smooth flow happens because people cooperate rather than compete against each other," concluded Dheeraj. "The same concept should be applied to teamwork too. Sharing the knowledge and allowing others to learn will increase the overall effectiveness of the team. If everyone on the team cooperates, together they can achieve more."

"By the way, Dheeraj Sir, did you see the Hindi movie - '3 Idiots'?" asked Nasreen.

"Yes! Nasreen," replied Dheeraj.

"I think, what you said about the competition is very well illustrated in that. The professor explains about the competition with an example of a bird; how it kills others to survive. I think it reflects the way most of us look at competition," said Nasreen waiting for reaction from Dheeraj.

"I guess so. Some of us are overly fixated about rankings. Yes, it is important that we do well in studies and everything else. However, becoming obsessive about rankings is bad. It is a good movie. One day, you should show that movie to John," said Dheeraj. Looking at John, Dheeraj continued "It is very important that we reward the right attitude. And it is also equally important to understand the fears, insecurities and get rid of them."

"Sure Dheeraj. I am getting a sense of all this. While reviewing the Build & Release process, I have noticed few things missing from the application. I am afraid my progress reports submitted earlier may not be accurate. I will get in touch with you after I go through it thoroughly," said John contemplating.

"No problem!" said Dheeraj assuring as they all stood up to leave the canteen.

___***___

The Meeting

Dheeraj was waiting for Prakash to complete his phone conversation. He came to Prakash's room at 5 minutes to 11 AM. He was quite excited about the scheduled meeting of that day. Throughout the night, he had been brooding over 'Competition versus Cooperation' and the impact of lack of teamwork on the community as a whole.

"Let's go, *Anna*," said Dheeraj as soon as Prakash finished his call. Both walked to the conference room with their notepads in hand. Vinod was already waiting for them in the conference room.

"Good Morning!" said Vinod.

"Very Good Morning Vinod!" both replied.

"Would you like to have some coffee?" asked Vinod, holding the phone and instructed someone on the phone to fetch their choice of beverages to the conference room.

After the initial niceties, Vinod said, "Dheeraj, Prakash told me briefly about your views on 'Best Employee' award. They are interesting. I want to hear more details from you. I'm all ears."

Dheeraj explained how that award might work against the team spirit. And he continued, "It is very important to look at the awards from employee perspective and how they perceive. Our good intentions might encourage negative behaviors inadvertently."

"I understand your perspective, but is it such a big issue?" pondered Vinod as he was perplexed with Dheeraj's concern. The practice of giving a 'Best Employee' award was going on for so many years. There were cases where people were unhappy with the selections, but no one had raised any objections against this award per se.

Dheeraj looked at Prakash as if asking for help. Prakash nodded his head in encouragement and gestured at him to explain.

Dheeraj cleared his throat and said, "I feel this is a major problem. Unknowingly, we have been encouraging our employees to compete at the expense of cooperation. We have the tendency to recognize individual contribution as more important than the team's contribution as a whole. The rewards should be defined in such a way that, it encourages team's success rather than individual excellence," said Dheeraj and looked straight into Vinod's eyes to assess his reaction.

Encouraged by the positive look on Vinod's face, Dheeraj continued, "When a team member is not able to do a particular work, if others help him, he might succeed in completing that work. A leader would love to see everyone achieve their goals. That message has to be communicated. And we should see to it that, the individual who contributes to the overall performance of the team should be highly recognized compared to the individuals who just excel at their work."

"I get your point, Dheeraj. I agree team spirit will help. But I don't see how not-encouraging-the-teamwork is affecting us?" questioned Vinod, still trying to understand the reasons for Dheeraj's concern.

Prakash joined the discussion. "Vinod, I was also a bit taken aback when Dheeraj first expressed his views to me yesterday. As a matter of principle encouraging team spirit is good. But, is it such a major issue as Dheeraj is making it out to be?" paused Prakash for a while and continued, "I brooded over it seriously and I am aware of the few incidents Dheeraj had pointed out to me. I think we as a community have been encouraging unhealthy competition all through the years. It has serious ramifications on the community as a whole."

"Community as a whole?" exclaimed Vinod and sat up straight in his seat. Dheeraj was aware of the change in the atmosphere and was happy to see Prakash elaborating on this. Dheeraj loved the situation where his views were elaborated by others, as it made it easy for his views to be accepted.

"I can give umpteen number of examples, how this lack of team spirit is affecting us as a community," said Prakash. "Take sports. Except in Cricket, India has not succeeded in any other team sport. There are individual claims, which can be accepted as individual achievements e.g. Chess, Shuttle badminton, Tennis, Shooting etc. Being a country of one billion, we should be getting more medals in Olympics. To win a medal at international competitions, we need great teamwork. And even in an individual sport, the support team has to show great teamwork to help the individual succeed. We should enjoy the success of our fellow-citizens, and should feel proud of them. If we encourage cooperation and excellence, we could win more medals in international events."

Realizing that Vinod was intently listening, Prakash continued, "As we know, we have two excellent sports persons, who have succeeded as individuals in International Men's Tennis. Every time we wanted them to play together to succeed in International men's doubles, there were stories of how each of them did not want to play with the other. This is one example of lack of teamwork. Recently, due to this we lost an opportunity to add one more medal to our Olympic medals tally." After a brief pause, "I personally feel this particular behavior is the biggest hurdle for India in overcoming the multitude of our problems and to earn greater respect in the world," concluded Prakash.

Vinod picked up the teacup placed by the office-boy in front of him and thanked him. There was complete silence in the room. Everyone was engrossed in their own thoughts. Noticing the sudden silence, the office boy left the room quietly closing the door behind him.

Vinod sipped his tea and started to speak out slowly as if spreading out his inner thoughts, "Now I see what you both are talking about. I can see how this one-upmanship, this unhealthy competition is affecting our everyday life. Individual's interests take precedence over the community interests. I can relate it to my personal experience. In our housing colony, we have to struggle to implement certain positive changes. People are willing to spend a lot of money in taking care of their individual houses. But when it comes to pooling money to strengthen the common structures, there is lot of resistance to contribute; even when the amount is very less compared to what they spend on their own apartment. In many instances, it is only a couple of thousand Rupees per house as compared to tens of thousands they spend on their house."

Dheeraj got encouraged by Vinod's comments and said, "Apart from encouraging people who contribute to teamwork, we should discourage selfish behavior. There are three things that we should watch out for and should try to set it right." Dheeraj stood up and jotted down the three principles on the white board and said, "We need to devise methods to communicate these principles effectively. It will pave the way for the common good."

"Very good, Dheeraj! Looks like you have done a lot of thinking about it. I understand your concern very well now," said Vinod and continued. "By the way, this topic reminds me of the story about Indian crabs. Have you heard about it?"

"What is that?" asked Prakash curiously.

"It is a very interesting story," started Vinod. "One importer of crabs received many boxes of crabs from all over the world. He notices that some of the boxes are not having any lids. Surprisingly, he finds all the crabs intact in the boxes and none of them jumped out. He is puzzled about the crabs not jumping out. He confirms that the particular consignment arrived from India. So he asks the exporter about this peculiar phenomenon. The exporter replies 'Sir, we know how the Indian crabs behave. So, we did not bother to put the lids on. Whenever one crab starts going up to get out, all other crabs will bring it down. The reason; every crab wants to be the first one to be out. So they don't allow any other crab to go out. In the end, nobody gets to go out.' That is how the story goes."

"It is highly exaggerated!" said Prakash disapprovingly.

"In one particular situation, this story seems to explain the behavior aptly," said Dheeraj. Vinod and Prakash have become fully attentive to hear what the situation was. "Take the case of traffic jams. I guess the crab behavior seems to describe it. Many of the traffic jams take place because everyone wants to be the first person to be out. In this process, none of them move forward," said Dheeraj.

"I think you are right, Dheeraj!" commented Vinod and continued. "I appreciate your effort in bringing this issue to my notice. I fully agree with your suggestions. It is too late this year to change any award process. I will instruct the HR team to review all awards and take corrective steps for the next year's Annual day. To bring real change in the society, we need to take similar corrective actions at the school level," said Vinod.

"I fully agree with you, Vinod," opined Prakash. "Anything we want to cultivate in society, the starting point is the school. The schools have a greater reach in terms of communicating and changing the culture. In India, even though our colleges have excellent standards in comparison with other universities around the world, our elementary education is lagging behind. Not enough effort has been put in terms of raising the standards and laying out a common syllabus for all the schools at the elementary level."

"I think so too," said Vinod standing up. "Thanks guys. It has been a great discussion. Dheeraj, I will instruct the HR team to constitute a committee to review all awards. You can be there on that committee to give your perspective."

Prakash patted Dheeraj on the back congratulating him, as they followed Vinod out of the conference room.

---***---

The Outing

"Sir, this is IMAX Theater," said Venkat after parking the Scorpio opposite to IMAX Theater. John got down from the vehicle and looked at the theater. It was a very impressive building. The letters "PRASADS" are standing out on the huge glass dome structure. Venkat also got down and accompanied John to the IMAX Theater. John came here to watch the '3 Idiots' movie with his entire team. He was looking around for them. He noticed Sanjay waving his hand at him. As they met, Venkat said to John "Sir, whenever you are ready to go back to the hotel, give me a call." And he left the place.

Sanjay and John looked around for others. They could not find any other team members. John was very impressed with the building and the surroundings. Entire place was well maintained. He noticed many people waiting in the queue for the noon shows. Luckily, they need not wait in the queue as they bought their tickets online. As it was hot, they decided to go inside and wait for others.

As they entered, a cold breeze greeted them. The entire place was air-conditioned and, it appeared like an enclosed mall. It had escalators, elevators and huge hanging posters of the movies. It was vibrant with lots of people talking loudly, laughing and enjoying. John felt it was much better than what the team had described to him. He was eager to explore all the other things available in that complex – the shopping area, the Fun Factory, Food court, etc.

"Hi John, hi Sanjay," said Nasreen as she approached them.

"Hi Nasreen," said both of them.

"How long have you been waiting? Where are others?" asked Nasreen. Before they could answer, they were surrounded by rest of the team members. As usual, there was noisy bonhomie with friendly jostling, hugs, high-fives and teasing. John noticed many people turning around to see what was going on. John used to get a little scared when groups of people behaved that way. Now he got used to the noisy and physical greetings. He also realized that every group minds its own business, and he had not seen any problems so far. John's attention caught an altercation between team members.

"What is going on?" asked John calmly, as he got used to the friendly bickering.

"Mallesh is questioning our decision coming here for watching '3 Idiots' movie," said Sanjay. "He says if we are not watching an IMAX movie, we should have gone to other multiplex theatres. He feels we are unnecessarily paying a premium price," explained Sanjay.

John looked at Mallesh. He was a down-to-earth guy and keeps a very low profile. Everyone in the team liked him. Only recently John came to know more about him. He interacted with him during the documentation effort of Sanjay's work.

"Did you tell Venkat when he should pick you up?" John's thoughts got interrupted by Nasreen's question.

"No, he asked me to call him whenever I am ready to leave," replied John.

"Ok. We have plans to see few other places after our movie. We can go there in Autos (the 3-wheelers). I will call Venkat and let him know the approximate time he should come to pick you up for the hotel," said Nasreen. While Nasreen was talking to Venkat, John was impressed by her concern to make him comfortable. He noticed that she always addresses Venkat 'Bhayya' – Hindi word for brother.

The jostling and teasing stopped only after they sat down for a cup of coffee at Barista. John was surprised to see the international chains in that complex. He noticed that Subway and McDonald's were also present in the food court.

They went to the 3rd floor taking escalator to get to the theaters. They entered the theater and settled down in their seats. Their reserved seats are all in one row. Ladies in the team chose seats next to each other, Nasreen sitting at the end. Sanjay sat next to Nasreen and John sat next to Sanjay.

That was the first Indian movie for John. He could follow the story and was enjoying the same. Nasreen pointed out the scene that she had referred in their discussion with Dheeraj. John thoroughly enjoyed the movie, especially he liked the songs.

"Thanks guys, it is a great experience. I thoroughly enjoyed it," said John as they were leaving the theater. More than the movie, he enjoyed the whole experience of it. During the entire screening of the film, the theater was electrified with the comments and whistles by the people. It was more like a stadium atmosphere during a football match.

"Hey, what is the next plan Nasreen?" asked one of the team members.

"Let us go to Necklace road first. What do you say?" asked Nasreen. Everyone agreed.

"How about having food here? John can have something at McDonald's or Subway," suggested Sanjay and looked at John for his reaction.

"That suits me," said John. He was already feeling hungry after sitting through a long movie.

All of them had some snacks at the food court. During that time Sanjay explained to John about Necklace road.

"I read about it," said John. "There is a large statue of Buddha in the middle of this lake, right?"

"Yes, that is true. Nasreen, are we planning to go to the statue?" asked Sanjay.

"Yes. We have to take the boat from Eat Street to go to the statue. Finish off your food fast! Otherwise, we end up going home directly from here," warned Nasreen.

Everyone got the cue and moved out of the food court. They came out of the IMAX complex and deliberated for few minutes, whether to take Autos or walk along the road. They decided to take Autos to the Eat Street – a popular place surrounded by amusement parks. They split into groups of three and decided to meet at that place. Sanjay, Nasreen and John decided to be in one group.

John was all excited. He had never been in an Auto. He felt them to be little unsafe - a three wheeler with no seat belts. At last, he was getting an opportunity now.

Sanjay hailed an Auto. Noticing John's uneasiness, they allowed him to sit in the middle. They had to squeeze in as there was just enough space for three adults. John was enjoying every moment of the ride.

They got down from the auto at Eat Street and were joined by the others. The place was heavily crowded. They made their way into the Eat Street complex to reach the water front. As they entered, John could smell Indian dishes. He realized that the food court had Pizza Hut, Baskin Robbins, Chinese stalls too. They went directly to the boat ride area. Unfortunately, the last trip to the statue already left.

They decided to spend some time in that area and occupied a round table on the side of the lake. They looked around and saw kids enjoying the rides in the adjacent amusement park. They could see the majestic Buddha statue as well as the Tank Bund on the other side of the lake.

Someone bought ice-cream for all. Few of the team members bought some food for themselves, but others except Mallesh forced themselves to share it. As usual, there was a friendly fight amongst them. John noticed similar fight while paying the bills. At every stall, they compete with each other in paying the bills. It was tough for the shop owner to decide whose money he should accept. It was a very unusual scene for John. So far, in that trip, he was not allowed to pay for anything.

"How about going to Birla Mandir?" asked Sanjay.

"What is this Birla Mandir?" asked John.

"This is a Hindu temple built completely with white marble," explained Sanjay. "We can see the temple from here. Look at that!" Sanjay pointed out the Birla Mandir to John. John turned around to see. The illuminated temple was appearing majestic. It appeared as if it was floating in the dark sky.

"It appears to be on a hill," commented John.

"Yes. You're right. The view of the city from that place is fantastic. Especially in the night, you will get a great view of the city. And it is a must see!" claimed Sanjay.

Everyone again formed into groups of three to ride the Autos. The ride was smooth for a distance of over two miles. After that, the Autos wound their way through narrow, hilly roads to reach the main entrance to the temple. The road to the temple was lined up with many small stalls on both sides. Most of them were selling memorabilia and material for praying. Some of the team members bought the material for offering to the deity such as coconut, incense sticks, etc. The complete structure, including the stairs and open areas was built using white marble. As they climbed the stairs, the atmosphere turned very serene. Everyone assembled on the open wide terrace. They decided to go on their own and return to the same place.

John went around the place for few minutes and returned to the assembling point. He saw Mallesh relaxing alone there on the marble floor. John had never interacted closely with Mallesh. Just recently he interacted with him in connection with Build & Release process. John wanted to know more about a particular step in that process. But, Sanjay could not explain the reasons and was blindly following that step all the time. When John asked for help, everyone in the team pointed him to Mallesh. Mallesh helped him understand the process and even reduced the total time for the process. He had automated many steps by writing scripts and brought the total time to less than four hours.

John looked at Mallesh. He was wearing his shirt un-tucked. He spoke English with a certain accent. He was the complete opposite of Sanjay as far as the mannerisms were concerned. In the initial stages, all these factors made John to ignore Mallesh. Apart from that, Mallesh appeared all the time relaxed – not busy. And he was in and out of the office on the dot, every day. Only recently John had realized that, Mallesh was an expert who not only finishes his work within the time but also helps others with their work. John realized how he faltered in recognizing the talent.

"Hi Mallesh! What are you doing alone here?" enquired John sitting next to him.

"Nothing! Just watching the beautiful night sky," replied Mallesh sitting straight up.

To start a conversation John asked, "Everyone is excited about seeing the deity and offering prayers. How come you did not join them?"

"I don't believe in all these prayers & rituals. If you do good, God will always do good for you," explained Mallesh.

The conversation continued about God, religions and social service. Both shared their views and respected each other's point of view. They stopped their discussion as one-by-one of the team members rejoined them. Everyone sat down on the marble floor and shared the 'Prasadam' – sacred food.

After a while, Nasreen suggested that it was time to leave. Everyone agreed. Nasreen called Venkat and asked him to come over to Birla Mandir to pick up John. They went down the stairs to the entrance of the temple. Except Sanjay, everyone left for their homes. Sanjay waited along with John for Venkat to arrive. Venkat appeared after ten minutes. John dropped Sanjay at the parking lot of IMAX theatre and headed for the hotel.

John was musing about the proceedings of the entire day. It was very refreshing. He felt very good about being treated specially by the team. Whenever he objected, the standard answer was "you are our guest." They did not allow him to spend his money too. Above all, he was glad that he got an opportunity to talk to Mallesh one-on-one and decided to meet Dheeraj on Monday without fail.

___***___

Change of Mind

On the following Monday, John went straight to Dheeraj's room. After greeting him pulled a chair and sat down.

"Dheeraj, I have been waiting all through the weekend to meet you and share this," said John leaning forward. Dheeraj nodded his head to signal go ahead.

John cleared his throat. "I made a mistake in selecting the right team member for the 'Best Employee' award. I want to replace my original selection with another."

"It is too late for that now, John," said Dheeraj. "I have already forwarded the selections to the awards committee."

John got disappointed and slouched into his chair. "I thought I could make this correction."

"By the way, whom would you recommend now?" asked Dheeraj.

"Mallesh!" said John. "I remember the discussion we had about teamwork and the need for recognizing the right behavior. Considering that, Mallesh is the best candidate," paused John. "I know more about him now."

"I see. What did you find in him?" enquired Dheeraj.

"He has everything that we wanted in a good team member," replied John. "Everyone in the team likes him, including Sanjay. He goes all out to help others, and he completes his work within the time. I could understand him well only recently."

"I see. Better late than never!" commented Dheeraj.

"He has great analytical skills and is an expert in writing scripts. He helped reduce the Build & Release time to four hours. Do you remember it used to take 2 to 3 days for Sanjay?" asked John.

"Yeah! You told me about that," replied Dheeraj.

"I could not recognize his talent. On a couple of occasions, Nasreen mentioned about Mallesh. But…" paused John. "My prejudices did not allow me to accept his talent. I was wrong in my process of evaluation."

"So, you had some preconceived notions!" said Dheeraj.

"Yes," said John. "I always gave importance to the outgoing personality and great English-speaking skills. Sanjay fit the bill perfectly. He is well-dressed and well-mannered. He stands out in the team as a person with whom I can interact easily. That created a bias. On the other hand, Mallesh is mild-mannered, down-to-earth personality. Until our recent discussion, I could not overcome my biases to understand individual team members."

"I am with you," comforted Dheeraj. "Each one of us has our own way of looking at things. Our culture has a strong influence on how we perceive individuals as well as situations."

"I guess you are right. I learnt a lot of new things last Saturday. I went out with the team to IMAX and Birla Mandir. It has changed lot of my perceptions," reflected John. "The funniest thing is that certain behaviors I considered negative turned out to be positive and vice-versa."

"Is that so?" exclaimed Dheeraj.

John sat upright. "Yes. It appears so foolish now. I noticed Mallesh spending time at other members' desk and thought it as a negative. Now I know he was actually helping them to complete their tasks. The second mistake is about Mallesh leaving office on dot every day. I know he has been completing his assigned work. But, after noticing people working late hours and working very hard, I thought he was not giving his best. Contrary to that, he was actually contributing a lot within the office hours than any other team member."

"I guess the aspect of working late hours made you nominate Sanjay for the award," commented Dheeraj.

"Yep," said John. "I came to know that Mallesh spends his evenings and weekends doing social service. He is a real gentleman – like the hero in '3 Idiots'."

Dheeraj smiled.

"By the way," said John, switching the gears "I need your help in understanding one other issue"

"Go ahead," encouraged Dheeraj.

"Recently, along with the Build & Release process review, we reviewed the entire application developed so far. The good news is that everyone knows the mistakes committed and how to avoid them in the future. The bad news is that we are falling behind the schedule as the mistakes have to be corrected," said John with a concern.

Dheeraj listened intently and asked, "Did you investigate what led to those mistakes?"

"Yes. The major cause is that of rushing through the development in the last minute. We realized that team members are over-committing. During the weekly meetings, we discuss the tasks and the team members give the commitment. Even though we have the estimates for each task, I allowed them to decide what they can accomplish in a week. I used to wonder how they can achieve the amount of work they committed within the 40 hours. During this review process, I have come to know that team members end up working late hours and weekends to complete them. I guess they were under-estimating the work always."

"Great analysis John!" appreciated Dheeraj to give confidence to him. "That could be one factor. But there is another important factor. Indians are not used to calculating the work in terms of hours. Rather it is taken for granted that the entire day is there for them to complete the work and not just the *eight* hours. When a team member gives his OK for the work, he might be thinking that he can work 10 hours or 12 hours per day. As we know *eight* hours per day can lead to productive work, but anything beyond that is not going to add productivity, rather it is going to decrease the productivity."

John was puzzled to hear this. "Why does anyone think that they have more than *eight* hours in a day?"

"In western countries a worker is paid based on the hours of work. And you have the concept of hourly rate" said Dheeraj and continued. "But, here in India there is no concept of hourly rate. The workers are paid daily wages. The Government here fixes the minimum wages per day."

"I see," said John.

Dheeraj continued. "The employees of this company are paid monthly salaries and there is no link with the number of hours worked. In a way, the salary is paid based on the number of days worked"

John was not able to see how it was related to the issue at discussion. "How does all this explain over-commitment?"

Dheeraj leaned back in his chair. "You see a workweek as 40 hours and the guys here see it as *five* days. So, what one can achieve in a day appears much bigger than what one can really achieve in *eight* hours. This leads to over-commitment. Things are slowly changing and especially in IT area people are more comfortable in estimating the work in terms of hours. It needs a paradigm shift."

"Ok. I get it," said John. "Now I understand it. I was excited that we were accomplishing a lot of work within short time. And in a way, I might have encouraged the team to over-commit. I will watch out for that and will force them to think in terms of *eight* hours per day."

John thanked Dheeraj and got up to leave the room.

Dheeraj also stood up. "By the way, are you participating in any sports for the Annual Day competitions?"

"Yeah! I am there in Volleyball and Ping-Pong," said John.

"Ping-Pong? Oh! You mean Table Tennis," said Dheeraj. "Best wishes John. Win or lose, enjoy your game."

"Thanks," said John and left the room.

---***---

Putting it Back on Track

All the team members, including Nasreen, were anxiously waiting for John in the conference room. John had called for a meeting with one-hour notice. Usually John gives at least a couple of days notice. So, everyone was wondering what the meeting was about.

The murmurs stopped as soon as John entered. "Good Morning team! You might be wondering why I called for this meeting. Let me get to the point straight. This is about TIME. And I decided not to lose *any time* in sharing my ideas about it."

Everyone relaxed a little noticing the tone of John.

John pulled the chair on which he was leaning and sat down. "I have noticed that many of you are spending long hours in the office, and some of you are working in the weekends too. I thank you all for the hard work. But, we are not seeing enough progress. Any ideas as to what is going wrong?"

John waited for the reaction from the team.

"We are spending considerable amount of time on rework," said Mallesh. "We need to control this rework. We have to get it right the first time. It will save a lot of time and we can make good progress."

John was happy to see Mallesh speak. "I agree with you, Mallesh. I am not sure, what is really causing us to get things wrong the first time. We can do that analysis some other time. But, I have couple of ideas to move in the right direction." John did not want to go into the details of overwork and how it is leading to sloppy work. He was careful not to hurt anyone's feelings.

"As I said this meeting is about TIME. First, I want every one of you to work only *eight* hours a day. No more late evenings and no more weekends." John stopped to look at the puzzled faces of the team members. "Let us get organized and give our best during these eight hours. Take your time and get it right the first time. As a rule, I don't want anyone to get stressed out working late hours. However, there might be few occasions I need your evenings and weekends. Let us hope we won't have to do that."

"Second, let us review the remaining work. Let us go back and re-estimate each task. We have to estimate every task in terms of HOURS." Turning towards Nasreen, John said, "Nasreen, I want you to keep the eight hours a day in mind and plan the schedule accordingly. Discuss with each member how many tasks they can accomplish in a week."

"That means, in 40 hours!" emphasized Nasreen.

"Exactly! Thanks for emphasizing that," said John. "Plan the weekly tasks based on what that particular team member can accomplish. It is unwise to expect everyone to deliver the work at the same pace. We are a team; and let us acknowledge the strengths and weaknesses of everyone. I want everyone to give their best and enjoy excelling. It does not matter who contributes more, what matters is how much we progressed as a team."

"I will have a detailed discussion with the team about remaining tasks and prepare the estimates," said Nasreen. "To complete the project in the given time frame, we might need more resources keeping in view this new rule of working only *eight* hours a day."

"No problem" assured John. "If it is required, I will ask for more resources. I would like to see very creative and innovative ideas from you all. Remember the way we have improved the Build & Release process. Maybe a brainstorming session will help in planning so that we can complete the project with the current resources. That is up to you as a team," challenged John.

Nasreen looked at the team for support and said, "What do you all say? Are we ready for the challenge?"

"Yes! Let's do it," said the team in unison. There was a new sense of enthusiasm and camaraderie. Nasreen and John felt great noticing that.

"One other thing I want to say about TIME," said Nasreen looking at John for approval.

"Go ahead," encouraged John.

Nasreen turned towards the team and cleared her throat. "As we have only eight hours to do the work in a day, it is very important that we maintain good control over the time. I have noticed on few occasions that we did not honor our time commitments. Being punctual is very important for us to excel."

Noticing Mallesh nod in approval, she continued, "Take for example, showing up in the office every day. And our flexible hours allow us to decide when we want to start our day in office. Every one of us should know when the other person will be in office. We should commit to a time and honor it."

"But Nasreen, it is not always possible to be on time due to traffic and other problems," countered Sanjay.

"I agree. That is a valid point," said Nasreen. "So what should one do in that situation?" Without waiting for an answer she continued, "The person should inform his leader immediately - that means at that first instance one realizes that he cannot make it on time. This allows the leader to take that fact into consideration and plan the day's activities accordingly."

John and the rest of the team were intently following the discussion. John was appreciative of Nasreen's efforts.

Realizing the mood of the team and with the newly found confidence, Nasreen leaned forward to elaborate her idea. "Being punctual applies to attending meetings too. It shows that you respect others and value their time. Punctuality is all the more important with reference to completing the tasks. We should agree on what we can accomplish every week – i.e. in 40 hours. If anyone realizes that he would not be able to complete the agreed task, that person should immediately – again I am emphasizing, at the first instance he realizes that – report it to me. How does it help?"

"It will allow you to have alternate plans," replied Sanjay. "You can provide any help to the concerned person to complete the task, or you can take any other remedial measures."

"That's correct," said Nasreen. "As a team, we can address any issues that person has, and together we can find a solution. I would like to see you all coming forward to share the problems & issues and seek help on your own."

"Excellent point," said John excitedly. "You are here in this project because of your strengths. No one is evaluating you now. I want each one of you to be open and share any problems you come across. Revealing ignorance, reporting problems and asking for help is not at all negative. Rather it is a very positive trait. We as a team should welcome these; and it will help us get to the root of the problems at the earliest. As you all know a problem solved at initial stages will avoid costly rework later."

John was happy with the way the meeting went so far. Nasreen asked the team to come for another meeting to rework the estimates and to do the detailed planning for the rest of the project.

John thanked the team, knowing that the team is on the right path. As they were leaving Sanjay said to John, "John, do you remember? We have our Table Tennis match today."

"Today? At what time?" asked John.

"6:00 PM"

"Ok, be ready for a tough game," provoked John with a smile.

___***___

The Last Mile

Weeks passed by. John saw the transformation in his team. The work had been going on at a great pace. The day everyone was waiting for has arrived – not the project completion day, the Annual day.

John was taken aback when he heard the name of the venue for the Annual day. It was Qutub Shahi Tombs. He wondered about having a party at Tombs. The company hired buses to transport people from the company to the Tombs and back. It was a mega event for the company. All the employees with their family members were invited. For the last few weeks, competitions were held for Sports & cultural events. The winners would be given prizes during that function.

John boarded a bus along with others and reached the place. It was a sprawling open space with picturesque landscapes. A big stage with a projector system was set up. Next to the stage, arrangements were made for the dinner.

John met his team members and their families. Nasreen introduced him to her parents and grandmother.

"Nice meeting you," said Nasreen's father to John. "Even though we are meeting you for the first time, it feels I know you for long time. Nasreen keeps telling us about you."

John did not know how to react. He just smiled and went back to sit with other team members. He watched the company presentation and enjoyed the cultural program.

He was glad that his project figured in the company's presentation as one of the important projects in that year. His project had made significant progress, in a week's time they would be making the final release for 'User Acceptance Test'.

The time came for the awards presentation. From John's team, John and Mallesh won awards in Table Tennis, and Nasreen won an award in chess. John was curious to know who would be the 'Best Employee'. The 'Best Employee' announcement was followed by a loud cheering. For good or bad, it was not Sanjay. The award went to a team member from another group.

___***___

Farewell

"Thank you all for the good words you have said about me," said John as he stood up to address the meeting of Project Managers. That meeting was convened by Dheeraj on the occasion of successful completion of John's project and as a farewell to him. Vinod was also in attendance.

"It is amazing how six months have passed by so fast. I cherish every day that I have spent here. I have learnt a lot in these six months both at professional level and at the personal level. I can tell you proudly that it is an enriching experience. To be honest, I had a lot of apprehensions when I was asked by Mike to work in India. All my apprehensions and fears vanished magically as soon as I met my *'Anna'* at the airport," said John in an emotional tone pointing to Dheeraj. Dheeraj acknowledged with a smile.

Everyone laughed at the reference of *'Anna'*, as this term is not used in the formal settings. John thought they were laughing at the way he had pronounced 'Anna'.

He cleared his throat and continued. "I owe this success to Dheeraj's constant guidance, from the day one to this day. He had given me many lessons in team building." He stopped in his speech and bowed towards Dheeraj as if to thank him. "Halfway through the project, I realized that there was a lot of discrepancy between the progress reports I prepared and the actual work done. To my astonishment, the actual progress is much less than what I have mentioned in the reports. I thought I would not be able to complete this project in time. Again, Dheeraj was at my rescue. With his guidance, I could understand what was going wrong and could correct the same. I could make my team cooperate with each other effectively and work as a team. Thanks to my team's commitment and focused effort, I could successfully complete this project in time. And I thank you all for treating me as one of you and for helping me feel at home." He bowed again, this time to thank all the participants and took his seat amidst clapping of hands.

Vinod waited for the applause to end and said, "John, I am curious to know what those lessons are. Can you please share them with us?"

John looked around to see if everyone was interested. He looked at Dheeraj and started to explain. "I guess these lessons are very specific to me as I don't have much knowledge of the Indian culture. You all might be already aware of the role culture plays in teamwork and how to adapt to it. I am not sure if the lessons I learnt from Dheeraj will add any new insights to you all."

Looking at John's hesitation, some of the Project Managers encouraged him to share them nevertheless. They said it might shed new light on team building as the ideas are being looked at from a different perspective.

John stood up again and moved towards the white board to face the audience. "I will try sharing the important ones. Interrupt me and ask questions if you need any clarifications. That will help me explain them clearly."

"As you know, this is my first trip to India - for that matter, first trip outside of USA. Initially, I had difficulty understanding people due to the cultural differences. The first problem I faced was interpreting the 'Yes sir' response. Dheeraj helped me understand that this response indicates respect rather than agreement. To elicit individual's opinion, we need to follow up with probing questions about their understanding."

"The next issue was related to work allocation. I noticed that many of my team members were not willing to take up particular tasks such as documentation. Dheeraj demonstrated very well how the tasks of everyday life are ranked. I came to know that the cause for this mindset is deep rooted in the hierarchical system of Indian society. And there are strong negative feelings about certain tasks. This knowledge helped me find workarounds to make every team member appreciate their work."

"The toughest problem I encountered and the greatest lesson I learnt is about recognizing the right talent. This is to do with my strong prejudice. To be honest with you, I gave greater importance to the communication skills and the external appearance at the expense of technical expertise. I was jostled out of this prejudice by a serious problem I encountered during the project execution. In the process of fixing that problem, I realized how each of the team members was competing against each other. And to my surprise, I was contributing to that behavior without realizing it."

"John!" a voice interrupted the speech. "What is wrong in encouraging the team to compete against each other? It will help each of them to do better than others and overall the productivity will increase."

"I thought the same," said John. "But, a discussion with Dheeraj and my own experience with the team proved that to be incorrect. What is more important is encouraging cooperation. I realized when individuals are competing, they were not sharing their knowledge, their expertise. They were possessive. They are all intelligent people; they know they can 'win' the competition by maintaining the lead. The logic is simple, keep learning and don't share."

John paused as he noticed the bewildered looks on the faces of the members. "By communicating that team's productivity as a whole is more important than individual's contribution, I could get my team members to share whole heartedly. I made it very clear that I would be evaluating the team rather than the individual. This created an open atmosphere for everyone to share their expertise without any inhibitions. And it has given courage to team members to share their problems openly. It helped us solve them early – you can say we nipped them in the bud."

"Wow! That is interesting," commented the same voice. Everyone else nodded in approval.

"The last important lesson I learnt is about the working hours. I was amazed at my team members' willingness to work extra hours and stay late in the office. I used to think, working late hours as a sign of positive behavior. As a matter of fact, I considered people who work late as high performers and encouraged that behavior indirectly."

John paused as he had noticed his audience look at each other unconvinced and surprised. "Until Dheeraj demystified this phenomenon, I was firm in that belief. On many occasions, I noticed the team stretching themselves out too far to accomplish a task by the deadline. I can tell you proudly that the work is completed by the deadline almost all the time. But, invariably, many of the tasks are completed only just before the deadline," said John stressing the words *'just before'*.

"If you can excuse me," said Vinod looking at John. Noticing that John paused for him to continue, Vinod addressed the rest of the team, "I think, we can relate this to the 2010 Common Wealth Games preparations. Just few days before the event started, there was so much hue & cry about the arrangements. At some point of time, the world had doubts about the event taking place at all. But…. "

Vinod looked around and continued, "But, the games started off with flying colors. There was highest participation from the world. Throughout the games and after the games, the same people who doubted the event's success poured encomiums on the organizers. The president of CWG federation declared at the closing ceremony that, 'Delhi had hosted a truly exceptional Games.' The next CWG host, Scotland, said 'it will prove a challenge to emulate Delhi's successes.' I think we have a pattern here." Turning towards John Vinod said, "Please continue."

"As you all know we at America monitor our work on hourly basis. A day's work is equivalent to *eight* hours. When it comes to fixing minimum wages, our Government fixes minimum rate per hour. But the Government of India, I was told, fixes minimum wages per day's work. The Unit of work time in India seems to be a day, unlike an hour as in America."

"How is this related to overworking by the team?" asked a member.

"Good Question," said John. "I had the same question when Dheeraj was explaining this phenomenon. As people tend to estimate the work in days, it leads to two issues. One, people tend to over-estimate how much they can accomplish in one day as a day has more than eight hours. Second, if the work is not done in the first two days of a week, they feel they can squeeze those 16 hours of lost work into the next three days easily." John paused to allow the members to figure out what he just said.

"This misconception resulted in some of them not being punctual and working overtime. As you all will agree, working extended hours regularly results invariably in rework. So, as a team we have brought the fact of eight hours a day into open. And we have planned all the tasks in terms of hours. And the team members are encouraged to review their accomplishments hour–by-hour. This helped the team to become punctual and manage their time effectively. As a result of this we have seen a significant increase in the productivity and job satisfaction. Thanks to Dheeraj and my team we have successfully completed the project on time. Thanks again to all of you for the constant support you have provided," said John emotionally and took his seat amidst wild applause.

Dheeraj stood up and thanked John for sharing his project experiences with the team. He turned towards Vinod and requested him to say few words.

"Thanks Dheeraj and thanks John for your insights," said Vinod as he stood up. Addressing everyone in the meeting, he continued, "I remember the three things that Dheeraj had mentioned to me once. For the success of a project, apart from encouraging people who contribute to teamwork, we should discourage selfish behavior too. There are three things that we should watch out for and try to correct." As he was completing the last sentence, Vinod walked towards the white board. He wrote the following on the board:

Watch-out and Correct

1. *Persons affecting others' performance negatively.*

2. *Persons who notice something going wrong and then not informing superiors, or not taking corrective actions.*

3. *Persons who are in a position to help a team member, but not volunteering to help.*

"Imbibe these principles in every walk of life and communicate the same to everyone around you. This will improve the quality of life in our society" concluded Vinod. Vinod then handed over a flower bouquet to John and wished him *bon voyage*.

Dheeraj thanked all and adjourned the meeting.

---***---

'Chalta-hai'

John was thinking about all that happened in the last six months. It had been a very exciting journey for him. Even though he faced many challenges throughout the project, he could overcome them with the help of Dheeraj. It was very nice of Dheeraj to have provided all that help. Without him, it could have been a very rough journey. Just a day before, John thanked Dheeraj profusely and shared with him the appreciation he received from Mike.

John felt the days and months passed by very fast. He was fortunate to have Nasreen as his team lead. She was very helpful and understanding. He thought of Mallesh, Sanjay and others too. They were all great and hard working. The lessons he had learnt from Dheeraj had helped him get the best out of the team. He made good friends of all of them. A smile appeared on his face when he recollected his apprehensions when he was asked to work in India.

"Sir, would you like some coffee?" the voice of the air hostess woke him out of his musings.

"Sure, thanks," said John and sat straight up in his seat.

John hesitated for a second and then picked up the coffee. He started sipping his coffee while closing his eyes.

As he closed his eyes, John smiled at himself recollecting the interaction he just had with the air-hostess about Coffee. He realized that he imbibed a few Indian cultural traits. When the Air-hostess had offered the coffee, he wanted to ask for a particular type of Coffee, but John said to himself "Chalta-hai" and accepted it. Earlier, he used to insist on his choice and only when it was not available did he compromise.

This was not the first time that John had said to himself "Chalta-hai" and compromised. Somehow he felt it eased his decision making, thus his life. When he first encountered this phrase, he had a long discussion with Dheeraj about it.

***

"Dheeraj, what is the meaning of this phrase 'Chalta-hai'?" asked John. "I heard it a few times while people were intentionally breaking the rules and on a few other occasions."

"Oh! You are a good observer John!" said Dheeraj. "This is a phrase in Hindi. It means 'take it easy', 'it does not matter', 'it's Ok' etc. But the literal meaning is 'it moves'. "

"By the way, tell me about the situation where you heard this," asked Dheeraj.

"Sure! I observed this phrase being used at work as well as at outside. The other day, we were in an Auto; the Auto driver took a U-turn in the middle of the road and started driving in the opposite direction. When Mallesh objected, the Auto driver said "Chalta-hai sir!" and kept on driving in the wrong way," narrated John.

"Oh! I see," said Dheeraj.

"A couple of times, I heard the same phrase from our team members also. I am scared of hearing that phrase as I realised that it is a form of justification for something that had been compromised," said John.

"You nailed it, John!" said Dheeraj looking at John approvingly. "Can you recollect any specific instances where your team members used this phrase?" asked Dheeraj.

"Sure," said John and continued. "I can tell you about two instances. The first is when I complained about the inconsistency in User Interface design. We had laid down very specific standards for colors, alignment of form elements etc; the templates for the forms were prepared painstakingly in detail. For example, the exact spacing required between two specific items on the form. When there were inconsistencies in the forms' layout, the team responded saying 'Chalta-hai John! It's so minor and it does not affect the functionality. So, what is the problem?' It took a good amount of cajoling from me to make the team correct all those issues."

"Oh! I see," said Dheeraj.

"The other instance was when we were about to make a Release of the application," continued John. "As you know, we do a complete Regression testing before we make any Release. Sometimes, we find a few issues - that show up in rare cases - just before the Release date. At that time we have two options, one to postpone the Release to fix those issues, another to Release the version as planned but highlight those issues in the Release Notes. Isn't that correct?" asked John.

"Yeah! That is the right approach," confirmed Dheeraj.

"But," John took a deep breath and continued. "Interestingly the team here always proposed the third option saying 'Let us Release this version as it is. The issues that we found can come up only in rare cases. Chalta-hai! Why unnecessarily highlight those issues? We will fix them in our next Release anyway before anyone can notice them'. Luckily, with the help of Mallesh & Nasreen I was able to convince them to choose one of the first two options," John stopped and looked at Dheeraj. In a mock challenging tone John said to Dheeraj, "I would like to see how you will explain this behavior."

Dheeraj smiled, cleared his throat and said, "This is a little complicated phenomenon. First, this phrase 'Chalta-hai' is used in many situations in different contexts. But overall the message is 'Whatever we are doing is an accepted behavior even though it is not correct. We can go ahead with it'. The underlying reasons are many, but they all are related in some way. Let me try enumerating them."

Dheeraj sat straight in his chair and leaned forward with an air of authority. "As you might have noticed, John, in our day-to-day life here in India we are forced to accept low quality service from various service providers especially the Government. There is no accountability for the service providers. Things are slowly changing now, but there is a lot that needs to be done and it has to be done quickly too. Added to this as I explained to you on many occasions, we are conditioned to become non-assertive people. With these two factors i.e. low quality service and non-assertiveness, we got used to the mind-set of 'Chalta-hai' and accept the delays as well as low-quality without making a fuss. This attitude of compromising helps us retain our peace or if you want to call it –sanity."

"Sorry, I did not understand what you said. Can you please elaborate?" interrupted John.

"Ok. Let me explain. For example, the water works department releases water every day for two hours only in our city."

"What!" exclaimed John.

"It might be a surprise for you that we do not get 24-hour water service, but that is the reality," continued Dheeraj. "Now during summer, we get water every alternate day and in some cases once in three days. What do we do? We accept. We adjust to the situation. We compromise and we tell ourselves 'Chalta-hai'. It is the same case with many other situations. Another example is electric power supply. It is reduced to few hours in a day during the summer. You cannot run your air-conditioning or fans. What do you do? We invent other 'cool' ways of comforting ourselves. Whatever resources are available to us at that time we try using them to overcome the problems. This way of inventing is called 'Jugaad'. This solution may not be a perfect one, but gives us some immediate relief. We tell ourselves 'Chalta-hai' and rationalize our solution as it provides the basic functionality."

"Wow! I heard about the word 'Jugaad' earlier. Interesting! I did not know about the water, electric power problems. I never faced those problems at this work place or at my hotel. I guess all of them have Power Generators. But why do our engineers have that 'Chalta-hai' attitude at work. They are the service providers here" said John stressing on the words 'service providers'.

"Good question," acknowledged Dheeraj. "You see throughout the adult life we have trained our people to accept low-quality services without getting agitated. In a way we have convinced them that it is the way-of-life. Don't fret, don't assert and just accept what you get to keep yourself sane. Take the instance of User Interface alignment you referred to earlier. Few spaces extra or few spaces less on a form is of concern to you. Now think along the mindset of our engineers – they ask 'what is the big deal? Isn't the functionality in place? The software application works without any issues. Then why are you so finicky about alignment?' Do you get it John?" asked Dheeraj finding John to be confused.

John wriggled uncomfortably in his seat, then stretched a little to get relaxed and said, "Yeah, slowly I am able to understand. But why do people say 'Chalta-hai' and break the rules such as taking a U-turn in the middle of the road?"

"That is one more interesting aspect of Indian life," said Dheeraj and continued. "The systems here are not always perfect. Rather I can say that only in a few cases they are perfect. So for a system-abiding citizen, sometimes it becomes difficult to get his things done. Take for example, in a city like Hyderabad, stopping the vehicle at a stop-line when the traffic signal turns red can cause a lot of inconvenience to others. And people look at you with indignation."

"I can't believe it. Why should following a rule cause that type of a reaction?" questioned John.

"Valid point," agreed Dheeraj. "It is valid only when the system is laid out perfectly. If you have observed, at many traffic junctions the stop-lines are not drawn at the right places. There are no proper standards for it. There is no consistency in painting the stop-lines and zebra crossings. So, in a way it is very ad hoc. In certain places - such as Tank-bund which is on the other side of Necklace road - there is no way you can cross the road if you want to strictly follow the rules. So people decide when to follow the rules and when to break them. Whenever they are in a dilemma, they say 'Chalta-hai' to themselves and break the rules."

"So, you feel the Auto driver taking an illegal U-turn is because of this?" asked John.

"Yes! Not only that, there is yet another factor," continued Dheeraj. "When many people disregard the rules, there is a tendency for others to do the same. So people, who do not do so, stand-out in the crowd. This calls for acts of courage and assertiveness from the rule-abiding citizens."

"I get it," interjected John. "The lack of assertiveness is again a major factor in this behavior."

"Absolutely correct," said Dheeraj appreciating John. "The major social problems are due to this. Take for example cleanliness, greenery, anti-corruption etc. – the 'Chalta-hai' attitude comes in the way of these reforms. Only when the people can say no to 'Chalta-hai' do social reforms succeed. For India to make all round progress the systems have to be well-thought out and the law-abiding citizens, who are the silent majority, must become assertive. That is the only way for real reformation."

"Excellent Dheeraj!" said John clapping his hands. "As usual you have explained this phenomenon in a broader context. But it seems to be a very complex problem to overcome."

"Yes. There is only one thing that can bring the desired change. All right-thinking people should become assertive. Almost all the time a few bad people dictate the terms for the entire population. For example, in our college days a few bad characters used to force us to boycott the classes, even though the majority of us did not want. The same continues to happen in every other sphere of life. For this to change the right-thinking people should become fearless and should say NO to 'Chalta-hai'," said Dheeraj. "Somehow we should train every citizen to become assertive. And these assertive people can bring in real good change in this democratic society," concluded Dheeraj.

***

John came out of his thoughts as he heard the announcement "Welcome to Minneapolis".

⌘⌘⌘

Acknowledgements

This book has been developed over a period of *four* years. It has been a long journey for me. The constant support and encouragement from my family helped me complete this book.

My father, late Sri Thota Durgaiah - a well-known High School Teacher - encouraged all of us to be open, bold, honest and humble. Thanks to him, all my family members reached great heights in education as well as in their careers.

Specifically, I would like to thank my brothers - T. Sudhakar, Lt. Col (Dr) T. Dayakar, T. Kishan Rao, Prof. Dr. T. Bhaskar Rao and Dr. T. Giridhar - for reviewing the chapters and providing feedback on the same. Special thanks to my brother-in-law Prof. Dr. M. Prabhakar for his unfettered confidence in me.

I would also like to thank my wife Kiranmai for patiently waiting for this event. Special thanks to my son Pratyush Thota for quietly listening while I was recording my thoughts for this book into the Voice Recorder. And a very special thanks to my daughter Sanjana Thota for converting Voice to Text. Lastly, thanks to my niece Vasavi Duvvur for the help in proof-reading.

---***---

About the Author

Thota Ramesh lives in Hyderabad, India with his wife and two kids. He is currently working at VJIL Consulting Ltd. as Global Delivery Manager. His primary forte is building high performing teams by motivating and training. His favorite topics include Behavioral Transformation for Executives, Project Management. He is passionate about sharing his knowledge to enable people to lead a happy life.

He received his B.Com from Kakatiya University, Warangal and M.B.A. from Osmania University, Hyderabad. He got his CQA certification from QAI of USA in 1995 and PMP Certification from PMI of USA in 2001. He is also proud of the "Competent Communicator" certification he got from Toastmasters International.

As software professional he worked in many countries, including Syria, USA, UK, Chile.

He is a keen learner. He learnt drawing and performing Magic & Hypnotism on his own. His sports interests include Cricket, Table Tennis, and Snooker. And he loves playing Bridge with his brothers.

___***___

NOTES

NOTES

Made in the USA
San Bernardino, CA
11 August 2015